Survival Strategies for the Holidays

Barbara Dan

[Scriptwriting professor 1996]

PUBLISHED BY

Eden Publishing
The Lakes, Nevada

EDEN PUBLISHING
815-1/2 N. Center St.
Newberg, OR 97132

ISBN 1-884898-08-4
Published by Eden Publishing, 8635 West Sahara Avenue,
Suite 459, The Lakes, NV 89117.

The cartoon on the book jacket was created by Dave
Moore of Minuteman Caricatures, Las Vegas, Nevada.

Author Appreciation to Carrie Dan and Clyde and Marion
Hedges for providing such valuable feedback and ideas.

Table of Contents

First published in her teens, Barbara Dan admits to enjoying a long and varied series of life experiences, including working as an actress, model, comedienne, singer/dancer, comedy writer, playwright, puppeteer, theatrical producer, publicist, fund-raiser, teacher, real estate salesperson, builder of houses, escrow officer, church secretary, dog breeder, publisher and editor, minister's wife (thirty-six years), homemaker, and—by far her most challenging positions—being mother to four now grown children and grandma to four lively young grandsons.

Besides degrees in Theatre Arts and Accounting, she earned her Master's Degree in Humanities from California State University-Dominguez Hills. She is currently writing her ninth novel. In spare moments, her interests range from trying to grow trees in the desert to historical research and making a better batch of fudge.

Chapter 1. Caught in the Undertow of Activity?

Some smart aleck put forth the adage that when you need something done, ask someone whose schedule of tasks already would choke a horse. The supposed wisdom behind this astonishingly insensitive theory is that this hyper-busy individual must know the secret of how to handle stress, work like a horse, and deliver on time.

The assumption behind this kind of thinking is that anyone carrying such a load of responsibility must have agreed to it and gotten involved in all this busyness because they *wanted* to. Because they actually *enjoy* being under constant pressure.

Oh, *really*! In my experience, such overburdened people just haven't learned to say "No!" Their lives are crammed with "shoulds" and "oughts." Everyone wants a piece of their time. At first this tends to flatter, but as the list of demands piled up, resentment and anger begin to seethe beneath the perky but frenzied little smile. Rescuers and nurturers are particularly prone to getting in over their heads. (You know who you are! Welcome to the club!)

The solution is not to blow your cork finally, or throw up your hands and walk out. The problem is that in needing to be needed, you have allowed yourself to take on more and more responsibility for other people. Pretty soon members of the family, intimidated by this dynamo of talent you have become, just settle back and let you take on the world alone. After all, you do it so much better than they do—right?

No wonder you're exhausted. And it isn't long before you begin to feel unappreciated. (Actually, your family probably resents you for taking over and shutting them out as much as you chafe over the fact that they have slowly dropped out of helping. It's a vicious cycle, and by November 1st every year, you are really dreading Christmas. You feel trapped. It's fun for everyone but you. You wish you could just book a cruise—*alone*—so you could escape from everything.

Only you can't. The budget's stretched, you never were a quitter, and so you grit your teeth and brace yourself for another marathon of Christmas cheer.

How many times have you asked yourself: "Why "*do*" Christmas, if it has become such an emotional and physical drain? Certainly what you've experienced as a frazzled Mom or Dad has little to do with the "peace on earth to men of good will" that the birth of Christ was intended to usher in. No wonder the love and joy of Christ seem buried beneath the tinsel and half-baked frenzy of shopping, endless long lines, office parties, and all the rest of the misery we associate with the tyranny of commercialized holiday ritual.

How do we do it all—at least the "important stuff"—without getting a coronary?

First, we need to recognize our limitations, our time constraints. Prioritize. Taking on more than you can comfortably handle is stressful, and stress is a real killer. Consider the medical statistics: Women who double as homemakers and bread-winners have finally gained near-equality with their male counterparts. Yes, by trying to do it *all* at the same time, women have increased their risk of heart attack and premature death. It is also not surprising that both sexes experience chronic depression, due to the added pressure of performing and living up to the expectations of co-workers, family members and friends during the holidays.

SURVIVAL STRATEGIES FOR THE HOLIDAYS attempts to help you reduce stress, regain your confidence and help you handle life better. The strategies outlined in this book will help you and your family maintain healthy eating habits while spending a minimum of time in the kitchen. Nutrition is at the forefront of your defense against depression, fatigue and feeling generally run-down. It's part of taking better care of yourself.

Every strategy in this book has been tested and works. As you take control of the situation, instead of letting yourself be inundated by tasks, you will soon get back in touch with your own needs and feelings. Your outlook will improve; you will feel renewed.

Yes, it *is* possible to have fun preparing for Christmas! You don't have to neglect yourself, or become the family work horse. By adapting the ideas in this book to your own situation, you can widen your circle of friends, develop a cooperative network, save money, and learn to savor the moment.

Years ago, my husband matriculated to seminary for three years of graduate work. While he prepared for the ministry, I worked full-time, rushed home to fix meals, clean house, and type term papers. "We" also had two babies during the last thirteen months of his schooling. I often found myself stretched beyond the point where it was "fun" anymore.

Occasionally I had the dubious pleasure of attending an on-campus club, dubbed "The Parsonettes," because it attempted to prepare wives of prospective ministers to meet the sometimes exhausting demands of a church congregation. Most of the "tips" shared by the seasoned ministers' wives who were guest speakers went right over my head. However, one idea managed to connect with my tired brain: A collection of recipes compiled by missionaries' and ministers' wives. Not ordinary recipes, mind you, but "bulk recipes" designed to feed a crowd of anywhere from twelve to a hundred and fifty people. (Nowhere near on a par with Jesus' feeding of the 5,000, but I was impressed!)

I latched onto those recipes like a drowning woman grasping a lifeline. Having those recipes stashed in a notebook gave me confidence that now I could face any and all challenges as a pastor's wife. (Boy, was I ever naive!)

Over the years, I confess to having used very few of those soup kitchen type meals, but I soon devised my own variation on the theme. By pre-preparing family meals and snacks for the kids attending the Bible clubs I taught, I saved *hours* that were better spent preparing Bible lessons. I also had more time to spend with my own four children and to devote to my writing, a lifelong vocation. This, I know now, taught me the value of time management and using the time saved to better advantage.

That is why I have put together this book of ideas and recipes. By the way, please don't limit yourself to the recipes in Chapter 11 of this book. You can easily double or quadruple your own favorite recipes—although I do encourage you to experiment and tempt your taste buds with a few new ones!

My plan for pre-preparing a month of recipes will get you through the harrowing, often frantic month between Thanksgiving leftovers and your family's traditional Christmas feast with a minimum of fuss in the kitchen. At the same time, you should be able to reintroduce a lot more *fun* into your life, as you try this new approach to an age-old problem.

The writer of Ecclesiastes [1:9] said, "There is nothing new under the sun." I agree. Ideas that solve human dilemmas get passed on from generation to generation. Many of my strategies are rooted in my intense admiration for the sturdy pioneer families of bygone days who settled this country. With their neighbors' help, they tackled Herculean tasks and accomplished amazing feats. This type of cooperation between families formed strong bonds of friendship and created a network of support that was absolutely essential to survival under rugged conditions.

Today, living in a society that is fractured and floundering for lack of extended family to fall back on, I regard this frontier spirit of cooperation as a healthy interdependency. There is much to commend it. The lack of connection is the common experience of far too many families and individuals today.

This fact was recently brought home to me when a woman engineer—a single Mom with a young son—expressed her frustration because she had no one close by to call on in the event of an emergency. (The last of her women friends had moved, and her parents and siblings live a considerable distance away.) Her situation is a growing problem for families, especially for single Moms and Dads.

During the Christmas holidays, this sense of isolation tends to exacerbate for many people. Often depression, a feeling of helplessness and of being overwhelmed sets in. But there *is* a solution, and people who dread the holidays needn't despair. Prevention requires prompt action, *before* the holiday blues have a chance to set in.

Families and individuals who lack a network of loving relatives and close friends need to become actively involved in a nearby church. Attend Sunday school and other study groups, not just the worship services. Meet people. Participate in potlucks, and cultivate friendships that will be mutually beneficial. Scouting, 4-H and other organizations also provide valuable social contacts, as well as supporting parents in the raising of their children.

When you move to a new community, take steps to find and meet compatible people right away. Don't settle immediately on the first person who makes an overture of friendship; take your time, and gradually build a network of friends who share the same concerns about child-rearing, spiritual values, interests, etc. That way, you will have a net to catch you when the need arises, and you, in turn, can provide the same moral support and practical help to others like yourself.

Reciprocal relationships can be fun and will add substantially to your sense of community and well being. They will lend a feeling of stability and security to other family members, as well.

SURVIVAL STRATEGIES FOR THE HOLIDAYS will help you create delicious meals for your family throughout the month of December with minimal effort. It shows you how to recruit family members, neighbors, co-workers, and friends. It helps you (and them) save money. However, its main purpose is really to create a network, even if one never existed before. Together you and your "team" of friends can bond, share laughter, pool resources, and get through the busiest season of the year without missing the joy and wonder of Christmas.

It is my prayer that, instead of waking up December 26th with a sigh of relief, "Thank God, Christmas is over!" you will awaken rested and with a sense of having been truly blessed.

—Barbara Dan

Chapter 2. Recognizing What's Going On and What Needs to be Done

Surviving the holidays sounds like the ultimate irony, yet many individuals and families see no escape from the frantic pace between Thanksgiving and Christmas. They work fervently trying to make the holidays great for everyone, but there is always a sense of let-down, disappointment, and depression. Yet every year the pattern is repeated. The demands of work, family, church, and various clubs and organizations we belong to just inundate us and lead us into a deeper fatalism and resentment.

So what *is* the answer? Are we going to have to keep repeating destructive patterns, or is there really a better way to do things?

First, let's examine what's going on. The holidays tend to overwhelm and exhaust us because a number of mistakes generally occur at the outset.

1. The entire family is not brought into the planning process at the outset. This prevents important input from being made by all members of the family, and also discourages their involvement. *SURVIVAL STRATEGIES FOR THE HOLIDAYS* will help you break this pattern of passivity.

2. Nobody has a clear idea what traditions, observances and events should take priority. School games, Christmas pageants and musicals often vie with other family activities, homework, chores, social gatherings, and church programs. Because a myriad of demands on time and energy and resources is involved, a calendar needs to be established.

3. Often, wrong assumptions are made about who will orchestrate and pull together all the tasks generally associated with Christmas. It is a real disservice not to let others know they are needed. Shared comradery and harboring delightful secrets can add significantly to the overall enjoyment of everyone during preparations.

4. In trying to gain more time for shopping, writing and mailing cards, sending gifts to out of town people on your gift list, etc., the first thing to suffer is nutrition. Eating on the run and snatch-and-grab munching can contribute to fatigue, snappishness, and a feeling of harried desperation. Sitting down at the table with other family members, even for thirty minutes of uninterrupted sharing, would have a beneficial effect and bring cohesion.

This is why menu planning plays such a large part in this book. It is not an attempt to cause people to "blimp out," but to maintain routine and bolster physical and emotional health during this busiest time of year. It eliminates having to come up with appetizing meals when you're strapped for time. It also gives the key planners a sense of control over the ongoing care of other members of the family.

5. Failure to plan and an inability to keep the whole question of gift-giving in perspective frequently lead to conflict and frayed nerves. Anticipatory stress over the January bills to come can lead to the steady deterioration of any holiday spirit or enjoyment.

Overspending is counterproductive and unnecessary. Careful planning and well thought-out gifts need not be expensive. The best gifts touch the heart and may be no more costly than a shared moment with a loved one.

6. Often people forget *why* they celebrate Christmas. The purpose of Christmas is not competition buying, or perfect decorating, or outdoing everyone else in the office with the originality of the exchange gift brought to the office party. Christmas is meant to unite people in a celebration of love, inspired by God's love, as manifested in the gift of His Son Jesus.

Every family has a different idea of what meaningful and special holiday traditions and activities they hold most dear. So before you launch into action, sit down with your family. Invite their ideas, and listen—*carefully*. What is really important to each? Make suggestions yourself, but try to avoid imposing. Also steer clear of doing things just because you've always done them a certain way in the past. If possible, incorporate ideas from everyone into your family's celebration.

Having established what the entire group wants leads logically to the next step: How are *we* going to implement this Group Decision? Wow! That puts a different face on the situation, doesn't it!

It means you're off the hook, no longer chief slave and pot scrubber. This is where you can delegate. It won't hurt at this point to confess your appreciation and how much it means to you to have them *volunteer* their help.

Before a counter-revolution can occur, you should divide each event or activity into smaller, less overwhelming tasks. This way you are not viewed as asking for the moon.

This is also a really good time to set up a Calendar of Events. I recommend a large office calendar of the type that each day has a space approximately 4"X 4" where all family activities can be entered and easily read by one and all.

Put it in a prominent place on the wall so that nobody forgets about it. Write down every ball game, party, church social, etc., that you have *agreed together* to attend. Avoid scheduling conflicts. If something comes up later, make sure it goes before the family for discussion. Some conflicts and events are inevitable, but you want to keep them to a minimum. After all, the purpose of pre-scheduling is so that the family can spend quality time together and also support one another in important ways.

Tasks related to scheduled events can also be posted. Whenever possible, indicate who is doing what, so that there is no confusion and no room for excuses later on. One of the hardest things to get from children and even teens is follow-through. By posting and discussing up-coming chores, tasks, etc., you will be teaching your children organization and responsibility. Because they are directly benefited by the activity in which they have *elected* to participate, they will have motivation and a sense of anticipation.

Plan leisure time just as carefully as you would save money. By pre-planning activities, you also prevent getting overloaded. Stress is reduced when the burden is shared.

Of course, not all chores can be shared. There will be times when you will want to enlist help so that you can work on a special project alone without interruption. Here again, your needs can be incorporated into the calendar.

Do you see what is going on here?

Consider: You are finally starting to acknowledge your own vulnerabilities, your limitations. By inviting your family's cooperation, you are also demonstrating that you feel perfectly within your rights to ask for their help. In the past, you have expended enormous amounts of energy in order to create a meaningful Christmas celebration for others. Including them in the planning stages signals a desire to assume a new and healthier role within the family. It also bestows on everyone involved the gift of mutual respect.

Chapter 3. Setting Realistic Goals

All May Not Be As It Seems in Paradise...

It is not always a given that every member of the family will feel thrilled by this new approach. Foot draggers are legion. Even when you break up the work into manageable tasks, you may encounter a residual rebellion. Don't be surprised when and if it rears its ugly head! After all, you have emancipated yourself by the startling decision to call a Family Conference. Even though you believe you came away from the bargaining table with their cooperation, you may have only gained lip service.

This revelation is most likely to surface when you begin to implement Project Christmas. Believe me, after dealing with four extremely independent teenagers, I know! One summer while selling real estate, I organized a program of chores and "fun" activities, so that we could expedite routine housework and spend more time swimming, taking short trips, and doing a variety of sports.

At breakfast the first day, I distributed a list of chores (a very short list) at 0800 hours. Since I anticipated chores would take no more than an hour, I spent that time on the telephone conducting business. When I hung up at 0930, I was struck by the unusual silence and went to investigate.

To my surprise and dismay, my two daughters were busy ironing pictures onto some white t-shirts my husband had bought but never worn. What kind of pictures? They were pictures of *monkeys*, each with an imbecilic grin on its face. My two sons were industriously crayoning pictures of monkeys in a coloring book. All four were deeply absorbed in their work and barely noticed my presence.

What these scamps had done, in defiance of my efforts to organize them, was buck the system. In retaliation, they had given my attempts to organize their summer a name: "Camp Chump," because in their opinion nobody but a "chump" would follow my regimen.

Well! I had a choice, didn't I? I could either lay down the law, or laugh and applaud their originality. I chose to do the latter. Their ingenuity, spunk and imagination won my immediate admiration. Who wouldn't prefer inventiveness and initiative over resigned acquiescence?

Besides, they were so happily occupied!

By the end of the morning, each one was wearing a t-shirt embroidered with "Camp Chump" and a grinning monkey.

My daughters also created a large pillow which has since become a priceless family heirloom. Gold fringed and made out of old sheeting, it sported the embroidered image of a mother gorilla surrounded by four loving offspring. There was no mistaking the statement made against their loving but overly organized mother. I could have hugged them breathless! Twenty years later, my oldest daughter is still the proud possessor of that pillow, which has held a place of honor on her bed all through engineering school and the raising of her own son.

My point is that some assertiveness and show of independence is to be expected. By keeping your sense of humor, you can probably transform a minor insurrection into a shared moment of laughter and love.

(In case you wonder, they finished their chores in record time that day, so they could spend *more* time getting back at me! It was definitely a win-win situation.)

On the Other Hand...

Delegating Responsibility Is Your Most Powerful Tool.

Don't Fight the Inevitable. Some traditions never die, or die extremely hard, so don't fight it. It's a waste of time.

I strongly recommend that you retain such customs and traditions as sending out Christmas cards or newsletters, because they keep you in touch with important people in your life. Nobody lives in a vacuum, and that includes you. If living halfway across the country from great-Aunt Sue intensifies your feeling of isolation, think how she must feel. That letter or card may be a lifeline for her, too.

But, you say, sending out Christmas greetings is so time consuming. Figure it out: Sending out cards will either take you three hours doing it alone, or you can recruit local talent.

The problem is to get the job done without the glue on all those stamps bonding your tongue to the roof of your mouth—permanently! Affixing return address labels is another job. And watch out for paper cuts from licking envelopes.

Solution: Assign stamping and closing envelopes to Junior. Give him a sponge and a bowl of water. Bribe him with a chocolate chip cookie, if he balks!

Hey, give him a cookie, no matter what. And in his hearing, brag to your friends about the terrific job he's doing.

Decorating the Tree and the House. Of course, you can go overboard on this. But you can't entirely avoid the subject. Christmas is going to come this year like any other, no matter what, so, stressed or not, you might as well plan on having fun decorating.

During the Family Conference, decorating should be one of the topics discussed. Do you want an old fashioned Christmas with ropes of strung popcorn, gingerbread men and homemade sugar cookies hanging from the branches? Do the kids want to try their hand at making paper chains? Or are we trying for a surrealistic look this year? —*Nah!*

Maybe you have enough ornaments from last year and want to put up the aluminum tree—or you decide to string lights on the squatty little pine tree in the front yard. Whatever the consensus is, set aside enough time to implement the plan. Let the decorations you use reflect what is most meaningful about Christmas to your family.

And remember, always follow fire safety rules. Creating an electrical short by loading on too many strings of lights is definitely not smart. Some of the nicest trees don't even have lights.

I remember one Christmas when my husband was a prison chaplain. We were living in a two room cabin on a ranch at the time, a temporary situation while we looked for housing closer to his work. Our girls were only eighteen months and thirty-one months of age. Because my husband commuted between two prisons in Southern California, the task of making a fun Christmas mostly fell to me. We were really strapped for money— almost as poor as the tiny grey mice who snuck out at night looking for crumbs in our minuscule kitchen. [Don't worry. I kept all our food in our antique refrigerator, where it was safe from contamination.]

I borrowed an old Singer sewing machine and made dresses from remnants for the girls. I also made them their first Christmas stockings out of felt.

Things were very tight financially, and I had perhaps $15 to work with. Having been raised in a fairly well-off middle class family, I can tell you I had certain expectations and knew we were going to fall far short of the lavish Christmases I had known in the past.

However, I also remembered that along with the presents, the trimmings, and the materialism that seemed so important to my parents, our Christmases was frequently marred by tension, outbursts of temper, and (even worse for us kids) a continual barrage of criticism and devaluing. Experience had taught me early that wealth, education and uncompromisingly high moral standards are not enough to make people happy. After eighteen years of passionate warfare, my parents reached the same conclusion and called it quits.

I firmly believe that my becoming a Christian and marrying a Christian who was also the product of a broken home—indeed, all the events leading up to my decision to embrace the Lordship and saving grace of Christ—were a part of God's plan for my life. As an adult, I felt no bitterness toward my parents, only sadness and compassion.

That Christmas, despite our financial struggles, I knew I was far richer than most. My life was bound up with three people who were dearer to me than any others: my loving (and extremely patient) husband, who needed my encouragement, and two precious daughters, who regarded everything around them in wonderment.

I *had* to come through for my girls. Fortunately, a friend went on a tree-cutting expedition with a church youth group, so we had a tree. It was tall and skinny, a regular Ichabod Crane of a tree, with spindly branches and brown needles.

Oh, my, I thought, looking at it from every angle and trying to decide which side of it *didn't* belong hidden against the back wall of the cabin. I don't think I had heard of Charlie Brown's tree yet, so I couldn't even derive comfort from that. Like many trees grown in an arid climate, our Christmas tree soon began to molt, even though it stood in a bucket and received plenty of water. But it was a pine, and it was free. What more could I ask for?

A quick trip to the 88 cent store and the grocery store helped some. The girls and I came back with construction paper, three rolls of party streamers, glue, a small vial of glitter, tinfoil, and popcorn. With these, a thick needle, and carpet-strength thread, we were all set.

Because the girls' hands were so small, I strung the popcorn, but they helped me paste brightly colored strips of construction paper until we had over a hundred feet of chains to drape around the tree. We fashioned a star out of an old pie pan and a few dangling ornaments, which we decorated with sprinkles and glitter affixed with glue. That glue bottle was like the widow of Zarephath's jar of oil; it just never gave out! [I Kings 17:16]

We baked a few gingerbread men and hung them on the higher branches, hoping the mice wouldn't find them. Next we used vegetable dyes to color slices of day-old bread stiffened with glue and cut into moons, stars, trees, smiley faces. [In those days the only kind of bread we could afford was day-old, but at 10 or 15 cents a loaf, I could spare a loaf for this very important project.]

In the days that followed, a pigeon feather and a few other lost "treasures" recovered from the yard were added to the tree. It wasn't long before the branches were completely covered.

We had so much fun inventing Christmas that year! The pride of accomplishment on my daughters' faces as they stood before the tree they had helped make beautiful is forever captured on film They each held a homemade stuffed animal, but best of all, they knew the joy of involvement.

Old-fashioned ingenuity really does pay off! I invite you to become part of this creative process as we proceed.

Chapter 4. Picking the Brain of A Shopping Genius

What should be our primary goal when it comes to Christmas shopping? **"No more panic in the malls**," was the first response from my own family's "fearless leader" and inveterate shopper.

When I asked my super-organized daughter Carrie for her input for a chapter on general shopping tips, I had no idea she had it down to such a science. "Born to Shop" and "Shop Till You Drop" do not even begin to describe the degree to which she has mastered this skill.

Your family probably has a Shopper, too. If at all possible, don't leave home without taking this person along. This person embraces the department store scene with the same aplomb with which some dieters clean out the candy aisle at their favorite grocery store. Only they find *values*, consistently and unfailingly, and they have an innate gift for knowing what everyone on their list will like.

Our daughter Carrie comes by this trait naturally. At sixteen she got a part-time job in women's fashions of a major department store, where she learned all the tricks of waiting until something went on mark-down and clearance. Her people skills and marketing know-how made her invaluable to customers. In a few months, she was the Top Salesperson in that department, and shortly thereafter, she was the best salesperson in the entire department store. She still made a pathetic hourly wage, but she had learned the retail business from the inside out.

To this day, if I need to buy something to wear, I take Carrie with me. Experience has taught me that I will never find what I'm looking for without her eagle eye. She can spot bargains on racks I have just pawed through. She can find colors and styles that coincide perfectly with the taste of whoever she's buying for.

Her advice to stressed shoppers? "Start early. Buy a yearly planner. Carry it with you. Use it."

Here are some of her recommendations.

Be on The Lookout for The Perfect Gift or Card.

If you're out shopping and run across a card or a gift that is absolutely "perfect" for someone, even if their birthday or Christmas is still a long way off, buy it—*now*. Don't wait. You will never find *the* Perfect Gift during December. That's when everyone else is on the lookout for great gift ideas and prices are sky-high. Buy it on the spot.

"Birthdays and holidays are predictable," Carrie would remind us—a fact that is so obvious that we often fail to notice! "They arrive every year at the same time. The Perfect Gift won't be there when you need it unless you buy it now!" You can save yourself a lot of frantic shopping for what often wind up being token gifts given out of a sense of obligation and time-pressure.

The perfect gift will mean much more to the recipient than something you grab off a rack during a last minute shopping frenzy when everything has been picked over.

According to every experienced shopper I consulted, December is the absolute worst time to buy gifts. What Carrie does is buy the Perfect Gift, wrap and tag it, and put it in a special closet for safekeeping. She files a "tickler" note to herself in her planner, under the month when she plans to give it, whether it's a holiday or birthday gift.

Buying Year-Round. "Buying one or two gifts a month spreads the cost of Christmas shopping over several months, so it's less stressful," Carrie says. As a single person on a limited budget, she has used this technique successfully for years. As a result, Aunt Carrie has come to be known as "Santa's best helper" at Christmastime. Her nephews can always count on her to buy the best presents.

Christmas Shopping in January. While we're on the subject of judicious shopping, it's wise to remember that shopping in December depletes your ready cash and diminishes your ability to take advantage of January sales. By shopping in January, you can save as much as 75% on greeting cards, stationery, ribbons and bows, and giftwrap. You may even pick up a few of next year's Perfect Gifts. If at all possible, budget some of your money for After-Christmas Sales.

My friend Marion estimates that she saves over $30 each year on wrapping paper, cards, ribbons, and Christmas candy, which she freezes and uses for Valentine's Day, Easter, and her daughters' spring birthdays. She recommends using the money you save to create your own Christmas Fund account. By taking advantage of discount sales all year round, you can accumulate quite a tidy sum for last minute shopping!

Both Marion and Carrie are firm believers in buying wedding and Christmas gifts during department store white sales. Try it, and realize your own savings.

Christmas Photos. When it comes to taking family pictures for those photo Christmas cards, put up a few Christmas stockings and trim around the mantle, and snap those photographs in October, so that you can order pictures in time to send out *this* Christmas. (If you think I'm joking, I have two very dear people on my Christmas card list whose Christmas snapshots consistently arrive in March!) It's all a matter of PLANNING AHEAD.

Speaking of which, address all your cards in November when you can add personal notes and get them stamped and sealed in plenty of time. The postman will thank you; your great-Aunt Minnie will be ecstatic. Most of all, your own family will appreciate the extra time you spend with them during the holidays, and the fact that you have avoided a shopping crisis, most of the charge cards are already paid off, and you are less grumpy than last year!

Bonuses and premiums: My daughter Carrie has shopping skills that leave me breathless with awe. Some of her gifts literally cost her nothing. She gets free premium gifts for purchasing film and many other products. As a result, she often has stuffed animals, stationery, jewelry, watches, and sporting goods items in her stash of surprise gifts for people. Don't *ever* neglect to send in for rebates! Coupons and free offers often accompany these. And don't forget, major credit card companies often reward good customers with bonus gifts—not to mention free travel!

Gift Certificates have the advantage of assisting the recipient in making purchases when department stores and other outlets run their yearly clearance of such items as appliances, electronic equipment, clothing, linens, and furniture. This is especially appreciated, when someone you know has a major item in the home to replace and wants to get the best price.

Anticipate what people are going to want or need. If Johnny is going to be six years old in August, he will probably need a good used bike. Be on the lookout! The same goes for computers; often you can pick up a good used one for $100-200 by keeping your eye on the classified section of your newspaper.

Consumer Reports and a number of trade magazines list which months you should expect the optimum value for your money on big ticket and popular new items, whether you're looking for cars, appliances or computers. Keep an eye on local throwaway newspapers and classified ads.

Tax-Deferred Education Savings Bonds really make sense when you're considering gifts for babies and small children. A small inexpensive gift will let the child know you esteem him/her; the bond will help the parents prepare for his/her future.

Bargain Stores. If your budget is rock bottom, but you don't want the kids to feel deprived, check out the Dollar Store in your area. Two of my grandsons have a bedroom stacked to the ceiling with plastic marvels and stuffed toys, because their mother knows how to find durable toys that are quite inexpensive.

Instead of buying Gramps another shirt when he already has a closet full, how about a few collar size-extenders, so his shirts fit around the neck again? (An inexpensive but indispensable gift found at most fabric stores.)

Don't overlook the bargains at thrift stores. When my husband was working as a Chaplain for the Salvation Army in Van Nuys, he frequently saw movie stars browsing through the second hand store. A lot of quality items are donated, including great ties, china, antiques, clothing, evening gowns, silver shoe buckles, and jewelry.

One of our Nevada State Senators, a woman who owns a number of businesses, loves big chunky jewelry from a bygone era. Guess where she finds it! She always looks like a million bucks, and being a Christian, she practices good stewardship of the material blessings God has entrusted to her every chance she gets!

Remember, wealthy people know how to use their money wisely; not all of them are tightwads, but they do avoid squandering it unnecessarily.

Garage sales and church bazaars are another place for astute buyers and collectors. You never know what gem you may turn up. One friend bought her husband a beautiful leather swivel chair in brand new condition for his office for $25. (At a nearby office equipment store, that same chair would have cost $200.)

Young couples might keep that in mind when furnishing their home for the first time. Children are going to scuff coffee tables and babies are going to drool, so don't put yourself in hock for years to pay off an over-inflated price on a new living room suite. You can put together a handsomely decorated home on a shoestring. Ministers' wives have been doing it for decades. In fact, I doubt our family could have taken as many vacations in the early years of our marriage, if we hadn't made it a practice to buy good secondhand furniture. The only time we bought new was when we couldn't find its equivalent in used.

Squeeze those nickels! It's nothing to be ashamed of, and you'll be chuckling to yourself all the way to the bank!

Caveat to Shopaholics. At Christmastime especially, people tend to go a little bananas. All the hustle and background noises at the mall tend to bring out a competitive spirit. Suddenly you feel as if you've got to do more and do it better than last year. You bought each kid on your list three presents last year, and naturally they're expecting you to do more this year, right? Hold on a minute! Since when did greed become compatible with the true Christmas spirit?

Harken back to Dickens' lovely tale, *A Christmas Carol*. What was important wasn't the fact that old Ebenezer Scrooge finally broke down and gave Tiny Tim and his family a Christmas goose—although they *were* hungry. What mattered was that Scrooge found out what was really important—people. Being connected with others in meaningful ways. When he opened his heart in *love*, rejoicing and true celebration finally became possible.

Love should be your foremost consideration in picking out gifts, or in making a gift. Some of the most precious gifts are intangible. For families in discord, expressions of affection and valuing will do much to lower barriers and enhance communications and understanding.

More Reasons Why It Pays to Plan Ahead. Why don't we take a brief look at some of the ways you can spend your time if you're not off plundering the malls at the last minute?

You might plan a weekend trip to the mountains, or take the kids to the zoo, an aquarium, or a Christmas ballet.

You might treat yourself to a "make-over" at your local beauty salon. Why not look your absolute best for the holidays? When you look great, you feel great.

You can stick an exercise tape into the VCR and work off a few inches over the next few weeks. Invite the couch potatoes in your family to join you. If you're out of shape, exercise for ten minutes, then work up to fifteen, twenty, or whatever you feel comfortable with. Getting the blood moving will improve your outlook on life and help you trim down without going through the torture of starvation diets. In four weeks, you should have no trouble getting back into that dress you've been hiding in the back of your closet, because you "outgrew" it last spring.

You will be able to give the kids more attention. Invite them to share what they did today. Learn to be a good listener again. (Don't panic if they seem to be having more problems than you thought. Getting things out in the open is half the battle.) They need to know you *care*.

Give and get a few extra hugs. Hey, who loves ya, baby? (Probably a lot more people than you think.)

Chapter 5. To Buy or Not to Buy

Should you buy gifts or make them? You will probably do both. Time factors often convince us we don't have time to make personal gifts that reflect an awareness of special interests of the recipient. By starting early and enlisting help, you may have a great deal of fun.

Let's tackle one of the major questions right away: What to do with that enigmatic male peeking out from behind the newspaper on the cover of my book. Is he really hiding out, incurably addicted to the sports page, or could it just be he's intimidated by your energetic frontal attack on Project Christmas?

As a member of the "gentler sex," he probably needs to be drawn out of his shell, little by little. Be assured, he very much wants (and needs) to be a part of the fun and excitement of Christmas. Men never lose that urge to be a kid, and I suggest you waste no time exploiting this fun-loving charmer when you need him most—at Christmas!

Even if Dad doesn't live at home anymore (in the case of separation or divorce), he may welcome the opportunity to get involved. If you can find it in your heart, invite his participation— for the children's sake. Goodwill with ex-spouses is important. It isn't necessary to make a big deal out of his helping. It doesn't mean you're getting back together. You just want to make Christmas nicer for the family *without* incurring undue expense. (Anyone paying child support will appreciate hearing that!)

Just remember the message of Christmas is "Peace on earth to men of good will" and bury past grievances. If you go about it with a right spirit, it may reduce tension over visitation conflicts all year round. Reduce the level of antagonism and watch your child blossom.

So if Dad is willing to cut out reindeer or nativity figures from scrap plywood, let him. He and Junior or Mary can paint them and even attach lights for a truly great looking lawn display. Watch the kids' social status in the neighborhood rocket through the roof after such an ambitious project.

But you may not be able to do anything that ambitious. That's okay. Try doing something else that expresses goodwill to your neighbors, if possible. Christmas is universal. Even people of another faith will enjoy a batch of cookies—and, yes, there is certainly no reason why Dad can't put on an apron and supervise the kids in the kitchen while you're out bowling with the girls from your office.

Another thing: Buy the children bicycles, wagons, trains, and other items that require assembly a few weeks before Christmas. This will allow time for Grandpa and/or Dad to take care of this without staying up all night on Christmas Eve.

Inexpensive Gifts. Ornaments can be made for people at the office as well as for relatives. Ceramic shops stock all sorts of unpainted pieces, which you can purchase. You will find lamps, ornaments, plaques, and much more. All of these make beautiful, inexpensive gifts with the personal touch and are a lot of fun to decorate!

Handwork. Think of all the great gifts you can

make with yarn. Shop the sales, stock up and spend commute time (if you aren't the designated driver in your carpool!) making those fingers fly! If you start early in the year, you can finish sweaters, scarves, mittens, "footies" slippers, an afghan for Auntie.

And if you doubt it makes a difference whether you make a sweater or buy one, let me assure you that home-knit items last forever! For instance, I knitted myself a soft rose sweater in two evenings (double yarn and #13 needles) in 1959. That same sweater was commandeered by my oldest daughter when she went off to college in a cold climate, and she's still wearing it. Compare that to the longevity of machine knits!

If you want to be remembered for decades to come and have a knack for handwork, consider investing some of your creativity in that direction. The same goes for crocheting. Imagine the beauty of a hand-worked table cloth—and the excitement of the person who receives it. One of my teenaged daughters crocheted herself an entire dress; I guarantee two or three balls of thread didn't cost nearly as much as a similar creation at Saks Fifth Avenue.

Finding the Time. All I can say is that you probably have more spare moments than you think, and if you take advantage of those snatches of time, you can accomplish a lot.

Years ago, while working as a teacher's aide, I used my 30-minute lunch hour to complete the coursework for a degree in Advanced Accounting. I could have spent my time stuffing my face and yakking about playground discipline, instead I chose to focus on a personal goal. A quick slurp from a milk carton and a peanut-butter sandwich kept me from physical starvation, but finishing my accounting degree proved infinitely more satisfying and led to greater career opportunities.

Whatever you set your mind to accomplish, you can achieve—if you are determined enough.

Learning A New Skill. Let's get back to knitting and crocheting. As a left-hander, I never mastered the intricacies of the crochet needle, but I know how to knit both the American way and the German way, which, incidentally, is faster because it utilizes the left hand to a greater degree.

If you don't know how and want to learn, ask someone to teach you. It is amazing how many shut-ins and members of the mission circle know how to quilt, sew, knit, and crochet. They are usually happy to share their knowledge. If, after asking around, you are still without a teacher, try the fabric stores or the hobby shops in your area. You may also discover other crafts you'd like to try your hand at.

Crafts not only save money and last, they are a wonderful way to work off tension, and they are a wonderful way to increase your personal skills and self-esteem.

Do you enjoy growing things? If so, consider the enjoyment a shut-in will derive from receiving the gift of a plant or spring bulbs. Have you ever noticed how much better a garden grows when a child is involved in the planting?

There are times when I have meticulously prepared the soil, planted seeds just the right depth, watered carefully—and never seen a single green shoot emerge. (Living in the Southern Nevada dessert doesn't help matters either.) I have also watched my grandsons' exuberant, extremely haphazard dispensing of seeds into the soil, and have been amazed to see a small forest of flowers and edibles sprout and flourish.

I strongly encourage any parent or grandparent to include at least one small child in family gardening projects. Presenting someone with a pot of daffodils, tulips, crocuses, or narcissus bulbs is an inexpensive but thoughtful gift, and it brings such cheer, announcing spring just when winter has worn out its welcome.

Fresh vegetables and fruits are always a welcome item, too; a basket of cheeses and items from your garden or fruit trees will make someone very happy. So will jams and jellies made during the summer and cleverly labeled with a whimsical rhyme and your name.

As your skills as a horticulturalist improve, you may want to learn the art of miniatures (bonsai trees). Every town has a floral designer who is willing to supplement his/her income by giving lessons. Discover another way to bring the outdoors inside.

Men and women may overlook some of the fun of using Shop Skills taught in Jr. and Sr. High school. Not everyone who likes to use their hands winds up being an auto mechanic or appliance repairman. Among the construction trades, there are many who use welding to build wrought iron fences, solder plumbing, and put together just about anything made of steel, copper, or iron. These talented people already know about safety when using an acetylene torch. Many have already tried their hands with creating works of art, such as jewelry, sculpture, toys, mechanized boats and planes, etc.

I recall an impressive sculpture of an eagle poised in flight that was exhibited at Caesar's Palace. (This was before they opened the Roman Forum, a wondrous place with many shops and galleries.) The eagle was made entirely of nails welded together. Its value in terms of materials was nominal, but in terms of artistry, it was awesome!

Who wouldn't enjoy receiving an original piece of art? Especially if it's made with the recipient and his/her lifestyle and surroundings in mind. The only thing that limits us is our shortened vision, our failure to recognize that each one of us has valuable gifts to give others around us. And the most precious gift we can give is our love.

Admittedly, many forms of artistic expression tend to make lone wolves of us. But there are many others that can be done in collaboration with others. Again, networking can reap infinite rewards! Not only can you create lasting friendships, acquire new and improved skills, but you can work together to create exciting gifts.

Many women I know get together year-round for a monthly Craft Night. By meeting for months before Christmas, they are not faced at the last minute with the prospect of Frantic Mall Mania, to which a large percentage of the population falls victim every year.

By the way, if you decide to form a network to create hand crafted gifts with a group of friends, you may wish to consider "bartering " two of your music boxes or a dog house for someone else's hand-tied and appliqued quilt or a hand-painted hobby horse. Find out what everyone in your group is really good at, and take advantage of the variety of skills and gifts produced by working together.

Have you ever considered creating individualized quilts that mark special events in the life of the recipient? This is especially exciting when a couple is approaching their silver or golden anniversary.

Maybe you'd like to start making a family quilt as a special family activity to be continued every year and detailing significant events, such as Johnny winning first place at the Science Fair, or Suzie being a cheerleader. Or why not commemorate the birth of a child? This is especially appropriate when we celebrate the birth of the Christ Child. While my husband was at seminary, eighteen babies were born the year my first child was born. (We all kiddingly said it had something to do with the plumbing in our apartment building.) At any rate, the network that evolved helped us all cope with the perplexities of caring for a first baby and helped a number of women continue to hold down a much needed job.

We furnished hot meals for the first few days after each new mother came home from the hospital. We also made ourselves available to the couple whose baby died *in utero*. Believe me, their sorrow was acute. They were a part of us, and we reached out to them in love.

We also exchanged babysitting, so that working Moms could rest easy about the care their child was getting.

None of this cost any of us money, a commodity most of us were short on. We prepared a little more food than needed for our own family's needs and shared it; that's all. (That's when I became convinced that cooking for a crowd is cheaper!)

All of us relied heavily on the seminary thrift store, which was stocked with layettes made by various missions circles in the Bay Area. We never met the women who were responsible for keeping our babies so beautifully clothed, but their efforts were a lifesaver. For 25 cents, we could buy an entire layette! (These consisted of a big fluffy quilt, receiving blankets, kimonos, nighties, bootees, and little shirts.) A dozen used, sanitized cloth diapers cost only 10 cents! [Be assured, I am still in favor of such economy, especially when I tallied it up and found out that a year's plastic diapers could pay for a good used car!]

Here is proof positive that networking need not be for personal gain, but for the joy derived from sharing from one's bounty. I am also sure that many of these selfless Christian women became fast friends for life as they banded together in a common cause.

Even children can do handwork. Weaving pot-holders improves hand-eye coordination and creates a useful object to give as a gift to a loved one. By eight, I was embroidering guest towels for my mother's friends bathrooms.

Don't neglect to invite others to share in the challenges you face. Networking gives people a sense of extended family. Parents and busy adults tend to neglect themselves and their needs in the day-to-day struggle to raise a family and keep up with life's heavy demands. Sometimes nurturing your creative side and including others has a healing effect. Set aside time to explore your own gifts and aspirations. Write a poem and frame it.

Always working for the Yankee dollar can leave us short tempered, feeling misunderstood and unappreciated; it may even precipitate conflict with loved ones, with disastrous results. Don't let that happen. Communicate. Share their burdens, and let them be part of your life. The results of such interaction may surprise you.

When it comes to gifts, wrack your brain and be inventive. For example, children can make a giraffe recipe holder out of a short dowel stick, a squeezy-type clothespin, a bit of plaster of paris, and a small plastic or styrofoam cup.

Paint it yellow with brown spots and—voila. Mommy's little helper has done it again, providing a way to hold her favorite recipes while she makes up a batch of cookies.

There are lots of books with craft ideas. One of the best I've found is Fern A. Ritchey's *Readers and Doers of the Word...The Fun Way* (ISBN 1-884898-02-5, $12.95) Not only does this book take a family through the entire Bible in one year without skipping around, it also provides over 365 Bible-related activities, arts, crafts, puzzles, ideas for service projects, parties, and ways to witness to friends. This would be a really good book to share with some of your friends at Christmas.

If you simply can't work a craft night or two into your schedule, or your skills are untried and you're hesitant, don't let that stop you! Grandma Moses didn't discover her talent until she was a member of the rocking chair set.

Let's not forget to do things during the holidays that nurture relationships. Encourage your kids to write their own skits and scripts and use a video camera to record the "TV show" for Grandma, who lives in Podunk. I guarantee that will be the best gift she receives.

There are so many easy-to-make gifts that children can create. One is a coupon booklet. All you need are an egg carton, 12 popsickle sticks, 12 cut-out flowers, a pencil, tempera or water colors, and glue. The child writes a different chore on each "flower" stem, such as taking out the trash, picking up toys, helping with laundry, washing dishes, or a free hug. Upend the egg carton, so that the popsickle flower can "grow" out of the bottom of each egg cup. Children have generous hearts by nature. They really delight in being able to give pleasing gifts.

Each year choose a family project, something that will help others. Donate clothes and toys to families in need. Sponsor a prisoner's child in the Angel Tree program and buy appropriate gifts; deliver them personally, if it's possible. Take your children with you; they're not too old to learn the meaning of compassion.

Make a family tradition out of reading stories with the children. There are many, such as Kenneth Taylor's stories for little children, or Barbara Robinson's delightful story, *The Best Christmas Pageant Ever* (Avon, 1972, ISBN 0-380-00769-X).

Take the children caroling. Invite their friends over for treats afterwards. (You might even want to videotape it and share the experience later with the grandparents.)

Include a new Christmas ornament in each child's stocking each year. That way, they will have a collection of fond memories and personalized ornaments to take with them when they are grown and have their own families.

One friend bought a bunch of Christmas molds (stars, trees, angels, birds, etc.) and used them to make plaster of paris ornaments, which the children painted. In later years, she used the same molds to form chocolate candies. Build meaning and memories into your Christmas celebrations.

A couple I know took their two daughters and donated canned goods, clothing and toys at a mission one Christmas. A homeless man received a sack of food; as he started to leave, he turned and handed back some of the food, explaining, "Someone might come in, whose need is greater than mine." Witnessing such an act of generosity and concern from a man living on the streets really broke their hearts. Often when we think we're there to give, we receive the greatest lessons in life.

Get a bunch of friends together for a multicultural progressive dinner. Include the children in the experience. Avoid having to drive long distances between houses. Give each other the gifts of caroling and wholesome fellowship. All of us would rather have the social time together than a bottle of ripe cologne.

So what if your first attempt at oil painting leaves something to be desired? It was still worth the effort. Working with colors and images and indulging a bit of time doing something just for your own enjoyment has value.

People tend to view themselves as having worth only when they are earning money or doing something for others. May I remind you of something essential to the re-creation of our inner spirit? When you love yourself and what you are all about, you will discover within yourself a greater capacity to love others and overlook their faults more easily.

Chapter 6. Wrapping Up the Holidays

"Wrap it up" is an expression that is commonly used to denote satisfaction or recognition that a task has been done—and done well.

The same goes for concealing gifts until the unveiling!

By now, we have (hopefully) picked out the Perfect Gift for everyone on our list. Now we have to keep them away from prying eyes and itchy fingers. The excitement mounts as the Day approaches. You notice Sally and Tommy whispering in the corner and giving the closet furtive looks and you smile.

That's because Christmas is for grown-ups, too, and you can hardly wait to find out what's in that lumpy box with your name on it and its green bow all askew. You wonder, but you're an adult. You have absolute and perfect self-control, remember?

Remember? Okay, so no fair peeking!

Seriously, wrapping gifts is a very essential ritual. I am sure the Magi wrapped their gifts for Jesus. As they opened their camels' packs and laid their treasure at his feet, can't you just imagine His eyes getting all big with wonder? Especially since he lived in a poor carpenter's family, where material gifts were almost unheard of.

True, the Magi rendered Him worship and adoration, but they also saw to His needs on this planet. Has it ever occurred to you what a truly remarkable thing their rich gifts were, considering that they were astronomers and aware of the vastness of the universe? It could only be because they *knew* this bright but unassuming Child was the "visible expression of the invisible God," and the great King of the Universe. [Colossians 1:15]   Do you think they would have risked carrying such treasures across open desert and rugged mountain passes where thieves and cutthroats lurked, if they hadn't been fully persuaded of their mission?

In the same way, gifts that minister to others in the name of the Child whose birthday we celebrate at Christmas are an appropriate part of our preparations and rejoicing.

Here, too is another opportunity for meaningful social exchange. Granted, some gifts will need to be wrapped in secret, but while the children are stringing popcorn in the living room or making fudge or caramel treats in the kitchen with their friends, a few of you Moms and Dads can do assembly line packaging in the den—and have great fun doing it, too!

Even assuming that none of you remembered to purchase wrapping paper, bows, and gift tags eleven months ago in January, you can save money by buying in quantity. The savings won't be as big, but it's still a great excuse for turning drudge-type work into a party.

Remember how last year you wrapped everything in embossed foil? Now you're faced with rising paper costs. (In some places wrapping paper costs rose 235% over what it cost the previous year, and it's going to get higher.)

Look for alternative wrapping paper and packing materials. Would it be so terrible if a really terrific present were handed to someone in a plain brown wrapper with a—forgive me, Charlie Brown!—yarn bow?   Have the children paint the paper with bright primary colors. And how about using a few of those freebie stickers that are given out as premiums with fast food combos? I see my grandsons wandering around all the time, securing colorful animals and smiley faces to the backs of chairs, the refrigerator, plastic toys, even the toilet tank! Collect a few of these gems and stash them for Wrapping Day. Start looking around you. It will surprise you how many ways there are to create original giftwrap without breaking the bank.

For instance, you might add artificial silk flowers, a sprig of holly (if you're lucky enough to live where it grows), or tuck in a bunch of sassafras roots. (Use a ziplock with simple instructions for making tea.) One friend of mine dehydrates rose petals and lilacs every summer, then creates the loveliest sachets and potpourri as an extra touch to include with a larger gift.

"Garnishes" on packages can be as inventive as you allow yourself to be, and add immensely to the fun and eye appeal of a gift. Even going out on a crisp fall day and collecting leaves, roots, pine cones, pinion or hickory nuts, berries or mistletoe can be a festive occasion with the family, especially if there's hot chocolate or warm cider and cookies waiting at home to warm everyone up afterward!

If you're like me, you have lots of odd, unmatched buttons. You save them in an old coffee can for the day when they will save you a trip to the fabric store. Over time the collection grows...and *grows*...and GROWS. You have all sizes, shapes and colors. You use a few white ones to replace shirt buttons, but the majority sit in the bottom of your sewing supplies forgotten. If you wait long enough, they will wind up in a museum after your estate is settled.

So why not do something really creative with them now? Let the kids create designs on the clean inside of brown paper grocery sacks, using glue and buttons, possibly some yarn or embroidery thread and a snippet of cloth. Other items might include macaroni, metal nuts (as in bolts), real or doll's hair, bristles off an old toothbrush—use your imagination! Create a caricature of the person to whom you're going to give the gift. Or "build" a house or car, or create a rural scene.

When it comes time to wrap the gift, just glue the picture on the box. Chances are the recipient will want to frame the picture, so don't go overboard with the glue to attach it. You may even want to protect it with cellophane wrap and/or back it with cardboard. I guarantee you, a gift this personalized will be cherished and remembered always.

Make small wreaths out of tiny pine cones glued to a cardboard backing. A bright red bow will ensure that the recipient will keep it to use in his/her Christmas decor next year.

By the way, if someone is really good at making bows, let his/her handle the final touches on each package (after the name tag is on the package, so there won't be any mistakes about who goes home with whose gifts). To avoid confusion, use large shopping bags or giant cardboard boxes, each with a family's name on it.

Meanwhile you socialize. You will be surprised how quickly you get through the pile and how effortless the wrapping process becomes. Stress is synonymous with 20th Century technology. Sharing tasks and laughter dissipates it.

In the past you've put off to the last minute making that trip to the Post Office, or UPS (or whichever shipper you prefer). Just anticipating those long lines and all the short tempered, strung-out people ahead of you puts a knot in the pit of your stomach.

Not anymore.

If you can afford the pick-up charge, you can even have curbside service from your home or office. (Check with the boss before you haul umpteen million packages in to work.) For another fee, there are also mail service companies that will box your gifts for minimal breakage. No guarantees, of course, but for *another* fee, you can also insure the package. And for those who drag their feet long enough, there is always overnight air freight.

However, all these extra costs are galling to many of us. We work hard for our money, and we don't want someone else making money doing something we can do for ourselves. All we have to do is get in the car and drive to wherever.

The trick is to get those independently manufactured gifts for out-of-towners into the hands of catalog and other 1-800 companies who ship direct. Send your gift cards separately and tell your friends to be on the alert for a package from such-and-such company. Practically anything can be purchased through such companies, but you need to be careful only to deal with reputable firms. It's best to select carefully, perhaps as long as two months *before* the Christmas rush and the elevated sales tag. Some companies will even absorb the cost of shipping, especially smaller book companies, who need your business to exist.

If you insist on fingering the merchandise yourself, by all means, shop your local stores with a critical eye for quality, price and *weight*. If you keep this in mind, you won't stress out at the postal counter, because the cost to ship exceeds the purchase price.

Wrapping presents for out-of-town delivery isn't as hard as it seems. Double-boxing is helpful when you have breakables. Small cushioned packages nestled in bubble-wrap, styrofoam "peanuts," shredded paper, or crumpled newspaper will usually arrive safely at their intended destination, if you use care and a sturdy outer box.

Remember, marking *FRAGILE* all over the outside only invites problems. Pack your gifts as if you *expect* a steam roller to run over it en route. If it's antique crystal, have the company you bought it from wrap and send it direct—insured. That way, the item can be replaced, if there is a mishap, and you won't wind up tearing your hair.

To finish up at the mail counter faster, make sure you have everything correctly wrapped and labeled according to postal regulations. Insure packages. You won't begrudge the extra pennies you spend, if anything goes wrong en route.

Another tip about getting through the marathon line at the post office: Go with a friend on a similar mission. Spell each other. While one goes to buy fast food for you both, the other keeps your place in line. (This comes in handy when a child or an adult can't put off making a trip to the restroom.) Believe me, the closer you get to Christmas the longer those lines are likely to be! Having a friend to keep you company will make the time pass more quickly.

By now, I'm sure you've noticed that many of my examples thus far have been drawn from low-end economic situations. That has been by deliberate design on my part. I hope I don't have to remind you that nobody ever became wealthy without knowing how to control their cash flow and make money stretch.

Besides, spending money is *not* the secret of having

a successful Christmas. Having fun while you're reinventing Christmas each year *is*. I don't want you to think pulling together Christmas on a shoestring has any inherent virtue in and of itself. It doesn't. What is "magical" about Christmas is watching what happens to the people interacting and scurrying around together to make it the most special time of the year. That can't happen if you're taking it on alone without help. That's why you *start* by enlisting help from the entire family. But that's only the start. There's more. By the time you finish this book, you will also know how to create a network that harnesses other community and neighborhood resources, to the betterment of *everyone* involved. (As opposed to welfare and other agencies that encourage dependency, this network will make everyone stronger, more confident, and more a believer in the "magic" of Christmas than ever before.)

Hopefully these ideas will serve as a catalyst for ideas, so that you and your family will see the possibilities and have a really jolly Christmas together. Don't just read. Sit down and brainstorm with your family and friends. And please write to tell me about your adventures in networking, etc. I'd love to share them with other readers.

Chapter 7. Networking Is A Must!

Networking: We've all heard the word. It's a byword that is much bandied about by "people in the know." Yet who really understands what it means? Computer junkies use it to refer to the online exchanges that hold them in thrall on the forums and chat groups. These "chats" tend to give lonely people the impression that they are connected...socially, politically, intellectually.

As valuable as such instantaneous communication is, in actual fact, the Internet can do very little to help us network with people where it really matters—in our daily lives.

Members of chat groups can participate in theorizing and spouting off about causes and solve technological problems, but when all is said and done, they still remain separate entities, often distanced by thousands of miles. Whatever information or ideas is exchanged, however useful, it isn't likely to make them function better as human beings.

Networking has been around since time began. But if it helps you understand the concept of interdependency and cooperation better by visualizing thousands of messages being bounced via satellite to invisible households, so be it. Personally, I would invite you to step back in time to when "networking" was extremely effective, non-technical, and probably more enjoyable. Since World War II, when families became more mobile and scattered, the art of human cooperation has been largely neglected. The power of these skills are not lost, but except for times of disaster, such as a natural catastrophe (flood, tornado, earthquake) or a war, a plane crash, or major tragedy, this heart-to-heart bond rarely surfaces.

But we needn't wait for disaster to strike to network. Once you have a fairly good idea what your family plans for Christmas are, it's time to call in the reinforcements.

Everyone has neighbors, relatives, friends, coworkers, a nearby church, local organizations they can tap into and call on in a pinch.

By the way, this book wasn't really written for people who live in a neighborhood of $250,000 houses, because most people in that income bracket can afford to hire help. But maybe that's to their detriment.

Some of the loneliest people I know rattle around in big houses. Everyone assumes they are happy, but money, as I've already mentioned, can't guarantee happiness. So if you happen to belong to this elite group, feel free to break loose from the expectations and tyrannies of conforming to your neighbors' ostentatious holiday preparations.

Find a way to touch other people in meaningful ways—and I don't mean writing a check for the down-and-out! You might want to do that, but how about also volunteering some of your time to help serving Christmas dinner at a rescue mission or a women's shelter from domestic violence? Why not visit the wives and children of prisoners? Volunteer your time at the children's cancer ward of your local hospital; spread a little Christmas cheer ...*throughout* the coming year.

If you do, it won't be long before you discover that you're part of an enormous "family" that really needs your compassion and friendship, not just a handout.

Now, back to the rest of us! Families that are intact, single parents, and even individuals without children (seniors and bachelorettes, for instance) can benefit from networking.

The intangible benefits often outshine the tangible. Example: A few years ago, every family on our block got together and, without spending more than $20, decorated every yard with Mexican-style lanterns. Perhaps 200 lunch sacks were partially filled with sand, and a votive candle placed each sack. They lined the edge of every lawn and both sides of each sidewalk leading up to the people's front doors. You should have seen the amount of light generated by this simple but charming display.

Night after night, we enjoyed the comraderie, as neighbors who were previously too preoccupied to get acquainted strolled up one side of the street and down the other, hailing each other and chatting like old friends. Such a simple idea created a sense of community sharing where none had existed before.

Since I already mentioned computers, why not post an announcement on the local online bulletin board and watch 'em respond! There are also groups for single parents—this is a perfect place to recruit members of your "team" so that, together, you can get through the holidays with a light heart, more energy, and a better feeling about your own competency. Wrack your brain. There are so many organizations and groups that you have only to check the community bulletin board in your local newspaper and contact a compatible sounding group.

Post a 3X5 card on your local church bulletin board. Talk to neighbors and coworkers who live near you. (It's easier if there isn't a lot of commuting involved.) Even if you are new in an area and don't know a soul, you can usually find others like yourself.

Drop by the local newspaper office. Talk to your dentist or your physician. Ladies, your obstetrician's waiting room is full of people who would love to network with you. (When was your last check-up?)

Any place where people congregate in meaningful ways is a good place to approach the subject of networking. (Forget football stadiums, ice hockey or boxing events, unless you or your kid is personally acquainted with the athletes and their families.) Get involved in the PTA and Scouts; talk to the leadership.

If you're a pet lover, contact the veterinarian and put up a notice on his board. Also, check out coworkers at the company picnic. They're much more approachable over a slice of watermelon than they are during a sales meeting.

Of course, you will take sensible precautions to weed out flakes, shirkers, and deadbeats. You don't want to bring anyone questionable home to meet your family. And probably the worst case scenario is someone showing initial interest but no follow-up; this type person expects everyone else to do the work. Drop 'em—*now!* You don't need more work, remember? Networking is supposed to be a joint effort. Make sure it stays that way.

The whole aim is to turn work into FUN for you, your family, friends and team members (soon-to-be friends).

All you have to do is form a bond of friendly cooperation around a common goal: Survival through the holidays. This is very easily accomplished:

Planning ahead. You meet, discuss, delegate, and implement the Plan. It's that simple. But it requires willingness and cooperation. Make sure you choose your team well. And don't forget to be a good team member yourself.

Sharing tasks. In order to have more quality time with family, this includes pre-preparing meals together, working on projects together, assembly line mailing and shipping. (The kids can help in many of these, with the added benefit that they will soon realize the value of cooperative effort, both among family members and between friends.)

Pooling resources through quantity discount buying. You can cut your food bill by 1/3 by using this method.

Selling the idea of interdependent networking will not be difficult. Everyone else is getting tense. By mid-November they already anticipate the crush of department store mania and the slow deterioration of relationships. Even before they plunge into the frenzy of Christmas shopping, baking, and decorating, they know what's going to happen. Just thinking about it makes their stamina flag beneath the daily round of keeping up with a job, household chores like laundry, cleaning, taking the dog to the groomer, getting kids to do homework... All this and now here looms that really relentless Biggie: keeping the family fed.

One more project, they threaten, and they may go berserk!

"But Christmas is coming!" Junior whines, with a calculating look at his already harrassed parent.

So you slouch outside to retrieve the artificial tree and ornaments from the storage shed. You start setting it up, and within ten minutes Sally has nearly electricuted herself. You find yourself asking, "Why, God? Couldn't you have figured out a way to send your Son into the world without causing such a commotion?"

Good question. And the answer is simple. Even at Jesus' birth, there was a network of helpers. Mary had Joseph, who found an understanding Innkeeper. (And probably a kind woman or two at the inn, perhaps even the Innkeeper's wife, lent a hand as midwife.)

And just to make sure everything was going all right for the young Couple, God had a few hundred angels hanging around. They got so excited about the Blessed Event that they had to share it with a bunch of simple folk in the area, Shepherds. If you reflect, it may seem odd that men who were used to birthing lambs would hurry to see the Christ Child, but they did. Even the stars in God's vast universe celebrated His birth—and eventuallly led the Magi across mountains and deserts to pay homage. Rich or poor, they came in humble adoration.

And regardless of how much merchants and others try to turn Christmas into a circus, we must never lose sight of the fact that history was forever changed by that one event, the birth of a Babe. Anyone who has held a baby or young child in their arms knows the magic of Christmas, the love of the Father and the care that was taken to safeguard the Child as He entered into the hazards of life.

That's why we never can say "No" when it comes to Christmas. Instinctively we know there is a child inside all of us who yearns for the Father's love, which was manifested in the entire life and ministry of Jesus here on earth. Through His sacrifice on the Cross, we can become new men and women inside! Christmas, don't you see, is as eloquent as Easter. Its message of hope embraces all people on the face of the earth. Because God sent his own glorious Son to live in human form as part of the family of a peasant carpenter, we are assured that He is also mindful of *us*, regardless of our station in life. His love is assured. And so we rejoice.

No matter how tough it is to keep up with everyday responsibilities, somehow we will find it in us to celebrate Chistmas.

So we network. We look for these people at church, at the office, at the supermarket, in our apartment complex or neighborhood, or at a parenting group. It's inevitable that you may find a flake or two among those you casually "interview." You pass over those who are looking for an angle or a way to use you. Deadbeats and freeloaders have no serious intention of paying their share or helping put the 30-Day Food Plan into action. Don't be paranoid; just watch for signs that you're being conned or "taken."

You aren't looking for deadbeats. You are looking for motivated people who are feeling the strain—hopefully you can contact them before they are very far along in their preparations. You explain that you have found this great way to keep from going broke during the holidays.

Once you've got their attention—because you will!—reassure them that you are not asking them to get involved in any multilevel marketing or bogus investment scheme. You are just a housewife (or housefather) like they are. Basically, all you're asking them is to consider going in together for the purpose of making holiday planning easier.

Since grocery shopping and preparing meals are time consuming when you can least afford to spare the time, you propose to work out a 30-Day Menu Plan. (One is included in this book, along with great recipes that will keep your family—and you—physically and emotionally in tip-top shape during the holidays.)

Here's how to explain the Food Plan:

You will all save money by buying in bulk. There are lots of wholesalers and membership stores that sell food in large quantities. Splitting up certain items will mean consuming it while it's still fresh and result in substantial savings.

You split the cost proportionately. The person with a family of six pays a per capita share, and so does the family with three. (No fair charging for infants, since they're still on baby food and formula.)

Once the groceries are bought, the team members get together for a couple of evenings or a Saturday of baking and pre-preparing meals, all designed to get you through the holidays. Using this method, the total time for preparing meals should be reduced to about twenty minutes per meal, without compromising quality or variety.

By cooking for large numbers of people, there is a savings in time and materials. Adequate portions will be divided up and put into ziplock freezer bags, containers, and taken home at the end of the Bakefest. It should take no more than an evening or two to do the baking and an evening of pre-preparing entrees.

(Preferably get two or three prospects together, so you won't have to explain what you have in mind very often. As they ask questions, you will generate much more interest by inviting their input. As the idea catches on, watch the enthusiasm grow!

The Food Plan is only part of the total plan, of course. Consider shopping If everyone has children who need/want jeans for Christmas, get the sizes and go have a talk with the manager.   There are enough wholesale warehouse type stores in mosts larger cities that you should be able to get a really good break. You may even be able to go to the factory outlet or a merchandise "club" and get extra savings. Teaming up also works if one person happens to work for a clothing store; employee discounts may be possible for quantity purchases.

By the way, one of the added benefits of the Food Plan is being able to buy from wholesalers and membership "clubs" without wasting food, repeating the same menu until something is (finally) used up, or risking freezer burn

Check the Yellow Pages for wholesale grocery outlets and restaurant suppliers. They're not going to turn away a good customer, just because she doesn't own a catering service. Frozen, prepackaged items and day-old bakeries offer products that can be substituted for a number of the items on the 30-Day Menu Plan. The whole aim is to save money, time and work.

Networking works for lots of things. It can put you in touch with people offering discounts with car rental agencies, travel arrangements, just about anything.

Once you get this network rolling, you will be surprised what other benefits you can get for your family. (Besides new friends.) You may want to use the concept and build on it all year round. Who says you can only pre-prepare meals during the Christmas holidays?

Chapter 8.
Strategy for Implementing the 30-Day Menu Plan

Once you have your network of people—you can involve as few as one other family, or as many as you can organize!—the next step is to put the Menu Plan into action. The reason all of you are doing it is to "buy time" each day, so you can devote more time to family and holiday preparations.

Keeping that in mind, you need to make sure all participants in the Plan are fully agreed as to what your menus will be. (Slight variations can be created within each family by the modification of side dishes, shifting or eliminating dessert items in the case of dieters, and individual preference for one bread over another.)

In most cases, it will be more practical if members of the Plan purchase their own family's bread products from a day old bakery. Buying for a month automatically will give them tremendous savings, and it's a big headache out of the way. Dessert items that are pre-prepared by the group won't compete with the type selections each family will make at the day-old bakery anyway.

Carpooling to the various bakery outlets and whole-salers can also save gasoline. If you decide to do this, just make sure you don't take a tiny car, because you won't have room to cram a month's worth of groceries for three or four families! A van or station wagon may use a little more gasoline, but it will eliminate having to go back to the store again...and again...and *again!*

At the initial planning session, the work can be divided up. If work schedules prevent shopping together—a missed social opportunity—divide up the tasks. Each person should inventory staples on hand (approximately). This is also an excellent time to clean the refrigerator.

Go through the Menu Plan and decide how much flour, sugar, beans, rice, etc., will actually need to be purchased. It's possible some of these items are already crowding counter space in canisters. Use what you already have before buying more. The price of a sack of flour or a 5# bag of sugar can be figured out. Ditto on cans of pumpkin, crisco, and spices that tend to sit in the cupboard behind stuff that's used daily.

Each person should pull these treasures out and add them to the collective pot. One person will have five pounds of dried pinto beans; another will have enough pasta or rice to take care of a crowd. Be creative and resourceful. Nobody is going to get ripped off in this cooperative effort. Everyone will bring useful items that can be incorporated into this culinary venture.

Caution: Cans that have puffed lids *must* be thrown away. Botulism is deadly. So is the careless handling of food. Everyone should wash their hands frequently during the food preparation. Cooking and baking at high temperatures will safeguard everyone from contamination. Fresh meats, fruits and vegetables not only make food taste better; they also keep better.

Keep in mind that summer berries and fruits can be dehydrated and stored in airtight containers and ziplock bags for use in making pies, muffins and breads during the holiday season.

Included with the 30-Day Menu Plan is a shopping list. You will notice that there are two columns. Many of the items in the first list are already on your kitchen shelves. If you have sufficient, there is probably no need to buy more. The second list mentions dishes you may need to buy for, if you follow the plan in the book.

However, there is nothing written in granite that says you must stick to the recipes in this book. If your "team" wants Mexican, or Italian, or Oriental cooking, modify the plan to suit yourselves.

You will notice that breakfasts are varied and packed with protein and carbohydrates to get your family off to a healthy start every morning.

I suggest you not skimp on breakfast. It's by far the most important meal of the day. You wouldn't start a car race at the Indy 500 without gas in the tank, would you? In the same way, start your family's engines with a tasty, power-packed breakfast that will get all of you past the mid-morning letdown that inevitably hits the light or no-break-faster. School teachers vouch for the improved scholastic performance of kids who eat a good breakfast. Productivity in the work place goes way up when people are running on a full tank of gas. (Oops! I'm not trying to make a funny; I'm still using the Indy 500 analogy, okay?)

I can see the raised eyebrows when you see the word "Dessert" following every evening's main entree. May I remind you that rarely is the entire family on a diet. Some of us—myself included—are on an eternal diet. (Not that it does any good, but I do try!) My point is, even if one or two of the members of your family is trying to restrict calories, that doesn't mean the rest of the family has to be punished. Deprivation is not what we're aiming for, but an upbeat, pleasant atmosphere at the table, which allowed sufficient time for sharing the day's events with each other.

This is especially important if you are not home every afternoon to greet Junior or Mindy after school. If you are lucky enough to have a flexible schedule and can be there, a cookie and milk are a must. I call it "Mom (or Pop) Therapy." Hey, I especially like the idea of "Pop Therapy," even though it's usually harder, for one reason or another, for employers to recognize the fact that Dads need to be there for their kids, too.

Kids thrive on sympathy and a hug. With today's hectic schedules, many children come home to an empty house. A lot of negative feelings about themselves can surface during those two hours before you get home from work, so be prepared to treat them kind of special when you get there, okay? I'm not talking about mushy sentimentality or you having a guilt trip. I'm talking about being a good listener.

Whatever else you do during the holidays, spend time listening to your child. Whether he/she is two or twelve, pay attention. **It's your job.** Your employer may not realize it, but your real job is raising responsible, healthy kid(s) who will make a contribution in society. Everything you do, every skill you bring to your employer's place of business is dedicated to that end. Your *real* job is taking care of your family—and that includes you.

That's why, during the stress of holiday preparations, a hectic work schedule, and the continuing demands of being a caretaker and breadwinner, you are going to take care of yourself. That includes getting to bed at a decent time, even if you have to shut off the television before the eleven o'clock news is off. It means you will treat yourself as well as you do everyone else in your family.

And for the month of December at least, promise me you *will* eat breakfast. It may surprise you how much better you feel, both physically and mentally. Taking care of yourself is a gift you can give yourself every day.

Try it. With the new lift in your spirits, you will find your internal "engine" burning off extra calories, too. Not eating or skipping meals actually slows down your metabolism. Sensible eating stimulates your entire system, so that you are less prone to colds, stress, and chronic fatigue.

It's Network Shopping Time!

Remember: You are not there to buy out the store. You want to leave with *only* the items you had on your list when you walked in. This means self-control. Lots of it.

You are, during the course of that forty-five minute sweep of the store, going to be tempted. Fight the urge. The Committee, or "team," already decided what to buy, and they are going to be very upset if you alter or add to the list of ingredients you have been authorized to purchase.

Now I know that busy people may not be able to shop at the same time. Whenever possible, however, you should try to do the major shopping with at least one other member of the group. Have everyone chip in a reasonable sum in advance. Otherwise you could become financially strapped by paying for the whole group's groceries. When you're buying for a 30-day period, that can wind up being a lalapalooza!

Another solution is to divide up the list and let several members help with the shopping.

In either case, it's very important to bring groceries *and* sales slips back to the group without delay and without dipping into the supplies for your own family's use. Regardless of whether you shop separately or together, this group effort will only work if you all play by the rules. I recommend you use coupons and double coupons; just make sure the brand name products you buy at a "discount" actually *are* cheaper than rival brands on the shelf.

Of course, if you can manage it, go shopping together. (One of you might volunteer to babysit all the kids, so that it can be done faster and without so much confusion.) Not only will you have moral support, but you can divide up the cost right at the checkstand. That guarantees that nobody will get stuck paying for more than their share. Money can make people tense, especially if they don't know each other well. Getting this issue out of the way right away will make everything else go more smoothly.

Of course, shopping together, you may wind up with everyone going off on tangents! That's okay if you take a vote on "specials" and "inspired" additions to the list. But it isn't fair just to spring it on the group as a whole *after* the fact. (The checker will also appreciate not having to referee a brouhaha at the checkstand.) What you are going to buy needs to be ironed out and decided in advance.

If you shop alone, make it fast, and stick to the list. *No deviations.* If you have to pick up a few other items like milk for your own family, set it aside until the group's list is totaled and paid for. Pay for your personal purchases separately, so that they don't show up on The List. That way there won't be any hard feelings among the key players in this time management project.

Time for the Bake-a-thon!

Schedule this either for a weekday evening or a Saturday, when you can *all* get together. Make it easy for everyone by suggesting a potluck. Unless everyone has a built-in babysitter, kids are welcome. (Better still, have someone supervise the kids at a different location. That way, you can avoid undue distractions from the smaller children. (You may want to involve older children and teens in stringing popcorn, making ornaments, or baking Christmas cookies.) If all the "team" members live in fairly close proximity, this should pose no hardship, and should the babysitter need a prompt assist, it would be forthcoming without delay.

Make it impossible for anyone on the "team" to exempt him/herself from being there to help. That is a cardinal rule. Everyone who signed up for the Menu Plan must share in the cost, the labor and—hey! admit it, some pretty terrific fellowship.

The Menu Plan is supposed to lighten the load for everyone. The first sign that someone can't find time in their busy schedule to help is when you divide the food and get on with it with those who *are* committed. Otherwise, you will find yourself being played for a sap.

Oh. I see. You don't like even considering that possibility. Well, face it: There is always that chance. You try to weed out "users" during the initial interview process. If a flake slips by you, try friendly group pressure. If he/she still doesn't roll up his/her sleeves, bump 'em from the program. That's the beauty of everyone buying (and paying for groceries) up front. If you shop together, everyone should come prepared to fork over their fair share at the checkstand. Boy, does that keep them committed to the project!

What to bring to the Bake-a-thon, besides a potluck dish, a babysitter and (maybe) the kids: Pots and pans, cookie sheets, pie pans, cake pans (with liners, if you have them), cup cake/muffin tins (paper liners, by all means), and big kettles, spaghetti pots, a sieve or cauldron to drain vegetables and pasta, large skillets, measuring cups, mixing bowls, a flour sifter, rolling pin, and seasonings. Put your name on the handle or bottom of the pans you bring, so you can keep straight who brought what at the end of the evening.

Bring whatever flour, sugar, brown sugar, molasses, baking powder and soda, and items you may have purchased for this project. Don't forget to bring a food processor and an electric egg beater. You might want to include a few big spoons and knives for chopping, unless your hostess is overstocked with such items.

You don't want to move in permanently! Just bring the essentials. Having to stop to go get something can be annoying, so come prepared to tackle the recipes you have all agreed to make.

Of course, ziplock freezer bags and freezer tape and paper should be in plentiful supply. As a general rule, baked goods should be cool before sealing them into freezer bags. You will want to have items that take awhile to bake in the oven in under an hour, so that they can bake and have time to cool before you take it home that night.

You will be surprised how fast the time passes. You and other team members and their families will be well on your way to becoming fast friends, if you aren't already.

And the pride of accomplishment as you stash your lovely booty in the freezer for later use is incalculable.

But we're not finished yet. Baking is only one phase of the Menu Plan. A major one, to be sure, including many breakfast treats and desserts.

In all fairness to everyone, take turns at different houses. This is why you will want to network, if at all possible, with people who live close enough. During your next get-together, you will be trying your hand at potentially the most delightful event of the day: Dinner.

Chapter 9. The 30-Day Menu Plan

Feel free to copy the Menu Plan and recipes that follow. They are designed to help you escape being a kitchen drudge during the holidays without resorting to junk food or wrecking your household budget by eating out every night. The short preparation time should also increase the amount of quality time you have available to spend with friends and loved ones, as you (collectively) reinvent Christmas with new holiday traditions, a more relaxed atmosphere, and that old pioneer "can-do" attitude.

Extra Tip: If you want to eliminate clean-up time, try recyclable paper plates, cups and bowls. I did this every time I had a new baby for the first three months, until our schedules became less hectic. Use any time saving device that you can think of. People, not projects are what count. That extra few minutes helping Junior with his homework, or helping Mary rehearse her lines for the Christmas play are much more important! Or how about a quick game of checkers with your spouse or a special friend?

In case you still have reservations about the 30-Day Menu Plan, let me assure you that I am not proposing that you compromise quality with potential freezer burn or mushy casseroles. There is no need to sacrifice good nutrition or eating enjoyment.

Have you ever wondered why diet plans that sell you most of the food are successful? It's not because the food is so terrific tasting. It's because most of us are extremely busy. If we had to do a lot of calorie counting, we would soon give up. These diet plans work because all you have to do is throw a pre-prepared item in the microwave and eat it. Of course, you are also required to consume enormous amounts of water to fill you up, because the dehydrated food and minuscule portions would turn you into a raving lunatic if you weren't so waterlogged that your mind is focused on frequent trips to the bathroom. (It's the truth!)

Don't worry. The 30-Day Menu Plan isn't going to turn you into a Spartan. It has the advantage of pre-preparation and pre-planned menus, but most of your daily menus will only include one or two items frozen items (usually desserts or breakfast items). Portions will be generous and satisfying. However, leftovers will be a thing of the past, thus eliminating the temptation to overindulge. Taking care of your body will lift your spirits. You will be amazed how much your family will appreciate the variety.

REGARDING LUNCH: The author assumes lunch will be eaten at school or the workplace; thus, it won't be included on the Menu Plan. Weekends: Serve soup and sandwich, or Hearty Chicken or Beef Pot Pie with crusty bread.

Drink plenty of liquids throughout the day. (That goes without saying. The Menu Plan only lists beverages once each day, but that doesn't mean you shouldn't drink them at every meal.)

Of course, whatever you decide about Christmas dinner is your business. The Plan doesn't even provide a menu, since every family has its own favorites. As my gift, however, I included a delicious stuffing that's been in my family for decades, because even when my grown kids have their own celebrations, they always manage to slip by for some of Mom's Turkey Stuffing.

Whether you use this 30-Day Menu Plan or make up your own, remember that basic to survival is nutrition. Enjoy!

REMINDER: People with serious health problems (high cholesterol, diabetes, food allergies, etc.) should consult their physician before trying out any new recipe or regimen.

Day 1 - MONDAY After Thanksgiving Weekend

BREAKFAST:
Orange Juice
Waffles and Syrup
Milk, tea, coffee (your choice)

DINNER:
Turkey Leftovers on Toast Points
with mixed vegetables and gravy
Head Lettuce Salad & Dressing

Dessert:
Ice Cream Cake

Day 2- TUESDAY

BREAKFAST:
Cranberry Muffins
Scrambled Eggs
Milk, Coffee, Tea (your choice)

DINNER:
Macaroni, Beef & Tomato
Casserole
Carrot Sticks - Green Beans
Whole Wheat Bread/LoFat Oleo

Dessert:
Frozen Strawberries & Shortcake
(Biscuit Recipe)

DAY 3 - WEDNESDAY

BREAKFAST:
Orange Juice
Instant Cream of Wheat
Toast with Jam, Jelly,
or Peanut Butter

(DAY 3 CONTINUED)

DINNER: DICED HAM & ESCALLOPED POTATOES
PEAS AND CARROTS - ROLLS & OLEO

DESSERT: PUMPKIN PIE (USE REST FOR DAY 5)

♦

DAY 4 - THURSDAY

BREAKFAST: APPLE JUICE
DATE NUT BREAD & HAM SLICES
MILK, TEA, COFFEE (YOUR CHOICE)

DINNER: STIR FRY CHICKEN OVER RICE PILAF
WITH MIXED VEGETABLES

DESSERT: INSTANT LEMON OR CHOCOLATE
PUDDING

♦

DAY 5 - FRIDAY

BREAKFAST: ORANGE JUICE
FRENCH TOAST
MILK, TEA, COFFEE (YOUR CHOICE)

DINNER: BROILED COD (OR CHOICE OF FISH)
MICROWAVED BAKED POTATOES
GREEN BEANS w/SLIVERED ALMONDS

DESSERT: PUMPKIN PIE (LEFT FROM DAY 3)

♦

DAY 6 - SATURDAY

BREAKFAST: CRAN-APPLE JUICE (YOUR CHOICE)
CHIPPED BEEF ON TOAST POINTS

(DAY 6 CONTINUED)

DINNER: BAKED LASAGNA WITH GARLIC BREAD
GARDEN SALAD & DRESSING

DESSERT: ANGEL CAKE OR POUND CAKE WITH
THAWED BLACKBERRIES & TOPPING
♦

DAY 7 - SUNDAY

BREAKFAST: ORANGE JUICE
SAUSAGE, PANCAKES AND SYRUP
MILK, TEA, COFFEE (YOUR CHOICE)

DINNER: BAKED CHICKEN WITH STUFFING
MASHED POTATOES (INSTANT OR ?)
CORN ON THE COB
LEMONADE - ROLLS & OLEO

DESSERT: CHOCOLATE FUDGE BROWNIE
TOPPED WITH VANILLA ICE CREAM
♦

DAY 8 - MONDAY

BREAKFAST: APRICOT NECTAR
OATMEAL
DATE NUT BREAD OR TOAST & JAM

DINNER: HEARTY BEEF & VEGETABLE POT PIES
WARM CRUSTY FRENCH BREAD
TOSSED GREEN SALAD & DRESSING

DESSERT: APPLE PIE
♦

DAY 9 - TUESDAY

BREAKFAST: BANANA BREAD
FRIED OR SCRAMBLED EGGS
MILK, TEA, COFFEE (YOUR CHOICE)

DINNER: MEATLOAF - MASHED POTATOES
PEAS AND CARROTS
BREAD AND LOCAL SPREAD OR JAM

DESSERT: HOME BAKED COOKIES

◆

DAY 10 - WEDNESDAY

BREAKFAST: APPLE JUICE
BISCUITS WITH TURKEY AND GRAVY
MILK, TEA, COFFEE (YOUR CHOICE)

DINNER: HAMBURGERS AND BUNS
MIXED VEGETABLES

DESSERT: FRUIT COCKTAIL W/LOFAT NONDAIRY
TOPPING

◆

DAY 11 - THURSDAY

BREAKFAST: ORANGE SEGMENTS
FRENCH TOAST
MILK, TEA, COFFEE (YOUR CHOICE)

DINNER: MACARONI WITH FRANKS OR
DICED HAM
GREEN BEANS
WHOLE WHEAT BREAD & SPREAD

(DAY 11 CONTINUED)

DESSERT: APPLE SLICES, OR 5 MIN.
MICROWAVE BAKED APPLES
STUFFED W/RAISINS

♦

DAY 12 - FRIDAY

BREAKFAST: APPLE JUICE
POACHED EGGS AND TOAST
MILK, TEA, COFFEE (YOUR CHOICE)

DINNER: HEARTY CLAM CHOWDER
CRUSTY FRENCH BREAD
LEAFY GREEN SALAD

DESSERT: CHOCOLATE CHIP COOKIES

♦

DAY 13 - SATURDAY

BREAKFAST: ORANGE JUICE
OMELETTE - GRAHAM BREAD
MILK, TEA, COFFEE (YOUR CHOICE)

DINNER: IRISH STEW WITH VEGETABLES
ROLLS AND LOCAL SPREAD
TOMATO-LETTUCE SALAD & DRESSING

DESSERT: CHERRY CHEESECAKE

♦

DAY 14 - SUNDAY

BREAKFAST: GLAZED COFFEE CAKE OR COZONAC
SCRAMBLED EGGS
MILK, TEA, COFFEE (YOUR CHOICE)

(DAY 14 CONTINUED)

DINNER: STEAK WITH MASHED POTATOES
GREEN BEANS - BAKED SQUASH
WHOLE WHEAT ROLLS & LOCAL
SPREAD

DESSERT: ICE CREAM CAKE

♦

DAY 15 - MONDAY

BREAKFAST: ORANGE JUICE
WAFFLES W/SYRUP & ICE CREAM
MILK, TEA, COFFEE (YOUR CHOICE)

DINNER: CHICKEN & HAM STRIPS CASSEROLE
WITH ESCALLOPED POTATOES
FROZEN PEAS - CARROT STICKS
TOSSED SALAD & DRESSING

DESSERT: ICE CREAM

♦

DAY 16 - TUESDAY

BREAKFAST: ORANGE OR GRAPEFRUIT SECTIONS
FRENCH TOAST
MILK, TEA, COFFEE (YOUR CHOICE)

DINNER: DINNER FRANKS & BOSTON BAKED
BEANS
FRENCH BREAD, OVEN-WARMED
LEAFY GREEN SALAD & DRESSING

DESSERT: YELLOW CAKE WITH CHOCOLATE ICING

♦

DAY 17 - WEDNESDAY

BREAKFAST: POTATO PANCAKES AND APPLESAUCE
                 MILK, TEA, COFFEE (YOUR CHOICE)

DINNER: SLOPPY JOE'S ON HAMBURGER BUNS
                 CORN ON THE COB

Dessert: BANANA SPLITS WITH NUTS & CREAM

♦

DAY 18 - THURSDAY

BREAKFAST: ORANGE JUICE
                 OATMEAL AND PEANUT BUTTER BREAD
                 MILK, TEA, COFFEE (YOUR CHOICE)

DINNER: LONDON BROIL, THIN SLICED &
                 COOKED WITH ONIONS, PEPPERS,
                 MUSHROOMS & SERVED OVER RICE.
                 BEET AND ONION SALAD
Dessert: CHERRY PIE

♦

DAY 19 - FRIDAY

BREAKFAST: GRAPEFRUIT HALVES OR SECTIONS
                 LEAN PORK SAUSAGES AND MUFFINS
                 MILK, TEA, COFFEE (YOUR CHOICE)

DINNER: CREAMED SHRIMP ON RICE
                 SPINACH SPRINKLED WITH ALMONDS
                 WHOLE WHEAT BREAD & LoCAL
                 SPREAD - CARROT-PINEAPPLE SALAD

Dessert: APPLE OR BOYSENBERRY TURNOVERS

♦

DAY 20 - SATURDAY

BREAKFAST: BRAN MUFFINS
FLUFFY OMELETTE, SLICED TOMATOES
MILK, TEA, COFFEE (YOUR CHOICE)

DINNER: POT ROAST WITH POTATOES, CARROTS
BREAD OR ROLLS

DESERT: BLACK BOTTOM PIE

♦

DAY 21 - SUNDAY

BREAKFAST: APPLE JUICE
WAFFLES W/ STRAWBERRIES & CREAM
MILK, TEA, COFFEE (YOUR CHOICE)

DINNER: BRAISED PORK STEAKS IN MILK GRAVY
PARSLEY POTATOES
COOKED CARROTS - APPLESAUCE

DESSERT: PEACH UPSIDE DOWN CAKE

♦

DAY 22 - MONDAY

BREAKFAST: ORANGE SLICES OR JUICE
OATMEAL - CINNAMON TOAST
MILK, TEA, COFFEE (YOUR CHOICE)

DINNER: SPAGHETTI AND MEATBALLS
GARLIC BREAD - GREEN SALAD

DESSERT: COOKIES AND ICE CREAM

DAY 23 - TUESDAY

BREAKFAST: BLUEBERRY MUFFINS
SCRAMBLED EGGS
MILK, TEA, COFFEE, JUICE

DINNER: PAN-FRIED LIVER W/ ONIONS & BACON
MASHED POTATOES
SLICED TOMATOES
BEET & CUCUMBER SALAD

DESSERT: SPICE CAKE (NO ICING)

DAY 24 - WEDNESDAY

BREAKFAST: ORANGE JUICE
SAUSAGE CAKES
PANCAKES WITH SYRUP
MILK, TEA, COFFEE (YOUR CHOICE)

DINNER: CHILI CON CARNE
GREEN SALAD W/SLICED MUSHROOMS
QUICK CORNBREAD

DESSERT: POUND CAKE WITH STRAWBERRIES

DAY 25 - THURSDAY

BREAKFAST: ORANGE JUICE
INSTANT CREAM OF WHEAT
OR WHEATENA
WHOLE WHEAT TOAST WITH JAM
MILK, TEA, COFFEE (YOUR CHOICE)

(DAY 25 CONTINUED)

DINNER: LASAGNA (BEEF OR VEGETARIAN)
TOSSED SALAD GREENS
GREEN BEANS - BREAD STICKS

DESSERT: VANILLA ICE CREAM OR SHERBET

◆

DAY 26 - FRIDAY

BREAKFAST: ORANGE JUICE
BROILED HAM SLICES
CHEESE MUFFINS
MILK, TEA, COFFEE (YOUR CHOICE)

DINNER: TROUT BAKED IN LEMON AND MILK
PARSLEY POTATOES
GREEN BEANS W/SLITHERED ALMONDS
TOMATO-LETTUCE SALAD W/DRESSING

DESSERT: CANNED SLICED PEACHES

◆

DAY 27 - SATURDAY

BREAKFAST: EGGS BENEDICT ON TOAST POINTS
MILK, TEA, COFFEE, JUICE

DINNER: BEEF OR CHICKEN POT PIES
CARROTS, BROCCOLI, CAULIFLOWER
WHOLE WHEAT ROLLS, LOCAL OLEO

DESSERT: RUSSIAN TEA OR GOURMET COFFEE
SERVED WITH COOKIES & ICE CREAM

◆

DAY 28 - SUNDAY

BREAKFAST: EGGNOG OR JUICE
SCRAMBLED EGGS WITH
HASHED BROWNS - BANANA BREAD
MILK, TEA, COFFEE (YOUR CHOICE)

DINNER: ROAST DUCK W/ SAUERKRAUT
DRESSING AND GRAVY
BOILED NEW OR MASHED POTATOES
BRUSSELS SPROUTS OR CORN
ROLLS AND LOCAL SPREAD

DESSERT: ANGEL CAKE WITH FRESH FRUIT

◆

DAY 29 - MONDAY

BREAKFAST: APPLE JUICE
BLUEBERRY WAFFLES, MAPLE SYRUP
MILK, TEA, COFFEE (YOUR CHOICE)

DINNER: SALMON CASSEROLE
MIXED VEGETABLES
WHOLE WHEAT BREAD &
LOCAL SPREAD

DESSERT: AMBROSIA FRUIT SALAD

◆

DAY 30 - TUESDAY

BREAKFAST: APPLESAUCE
CHOCOLATE CHIP PANCAKES & SYRUP
MILK, TEA, COFFEE (YOUR CHOICE)

	(DAY 30 CONTINUED)
DINNER:	BROILED HAM STEAKS
	SWEET POTATOES AND CORN
	LEAFY GREEN SALAD & DRESSING
	ROLLS & LOCAL SPREAD

DESSERT:	APPLE PIE

◆

 *Don't forget...*

Children love snacks. My family likes butterscotch brownies, pumpkin bars, chocolate chip and peanut butter cookies, and snickerdoodles. Most cook books have tons of cookie recipes. Get the children involved making your family favorites. Share them with neighbors and friends.

Happy Holidays!

Chapter 10. Inventory and Shopping Checklists

Before shopping, members of the co-op should check their current food supplies on hand. It doesn't take that long—really! In most cases, you already know what you have and don't have in the cupboard. If you don't it won't hurt to find out! You may be surprised how much you haven't used in the frenzy to take care of all the other demands of a busy life.

The checklists provided will help you quickly inventory supplies. The Stock List will help you consider present inventory, as well as store items that you will need to accomplish your goal with a minimum of effort. Items on the Pre-Prepare List are there to jog your memory and help you quickly recognize what needs to be purchased, and what is already available on your kitchen shelves.

You will notice that not all pre-prepared menu items need to be made by the cooperative network you set up; only a few. Anything you can pre-prepare *cheaper* than the store sells it is something to consider. Sometimes it's just not worth the extra time and effort, but many times it will really pay off in a big way.

For instance, if someone in the group knows how to put a no-stick waffle iron to good use, he/she may want to prepare enough for the whole gang. After all, the main ingredient is flour. On the other hand, if you can a huge package, you may be expending energy that could be better spent making chocolate fudge brownies as rewards for an army of kids. (Notice, I didn't say Mom or Dad has to pig out on brownies, but most kids will have no trouble burning off a few extra calories. And, oh, my, will they ever "rise up and call you blessed"! [Proverbs 31:28] The whole aim of good cooking is to keep 'em happy, because then you're happy, right? (Right.)

Because it's likely that you and the other members of the cooperative network will substitute some of your own favorite recipes, the changes you make will alter what your group's actual list will contain. Remember, nothing is set in cement. These lists are intended merely to help you see what may need to be purchased and what can be utilized out of present food supplies.

Another thing, don't be overwhelmed by the number of items on the list. It might surprise you how many items you would write down, if you took everything out of your cupboards and made a complete inventory. No one is asking you to do that! Just use it to create your own network's list.

If the ingredients in any recipe seem too expensive, substitute another recipe, or use a reasonable substitute for a major ingredient. In other words, if canned salmon costs too much, there is no reason you can't substitute tuna, mackerel or deboned chicken. This menu plan is meant to *help* you, not put you into another bind.

You know your family better than anyone. If there's no way they will eat a particular item, serve something they like.

The breakfast cereals are all economical, but if little round Os rule at your house and you don't mind the extra cost, scratch the instant oatmeal, whole wheat and cream of wheat. You won't save any time, but if it makes for happy campers, so be it.

If you prefer to serve tuna casserole three times a week and can get away with it (!) without causing a family insurrection, who am I to argue with your decision. All I can say is, use good sense, give your family a healthy variety of foods, and spend the time saved in the kitchen to cultivate closer relationships with family and friends.

REMEMBER
The Menu Plan is not the primary goal;
only a means to an end.

80

Grocery Check Lists

Already Stocked?

Ziplock Bags
Foil
Freezer Paper
Freezer tape
Onions, Garlic, Celery
Frozen Juices
  Apple
  Cranberry
  Orange
  Lemonade
Frozen Strawberries
Frozen Blueberries
French Toast, frozen
Frozen Waffles
Instant Puddings
  Chocolate
  Lemon
Cake Mixes
  Yellow Cake
  Lemon Cake
  Spice Cake
  Chocolate Cake
  Pound Cake or Angel Cake
Brownie Mix
Unsweetened Bakers Chocolate
Peanut Butter
Jelly/Jam/Preserves
Pancake Syrup
Biscuit/Pancake/Waffle Mix
Macaroni
Noodles
Spaghetti
Lasagna
Rice
Wild Rice
Potatoes

Oatmeal, Instant (box)
Wheatena
Cream of Wheat
Dry Cereal (use it up!)

Canned Soups for quick casseroles
  Tomato
  Mushroom
  Celery
  Cheese Soup/Sauce
  Bouillon Cubes: Beef/Chicken

Chocolate Syrup
Whipped Topping
Salad Dressings

Chocolate Chips
Slivered or broken Nuts
Dried Dates, Figs or Apricots
Raisins
Shredded Coconut
Marshmallows

Applesauce, canned
Fruit cocktail, canned
Crushed Pineapple, canned
Canned or Frozen Vegetables
  Green Beans
  Peas and Carrots
  Corn
  Canned Beets
  Canned Sauerkraut
  Canned Spinach
  Canned Yams/Sweet Potatoes
  Canned Pumpkin

Already Stocked: (continued)	Items to Pre-Prepare or

Already Stocked: (continued)
Flour
Whole Wheat or Graham Flour
Baking Soda
Baking Powder
Brown Sugar
Powdered Sugar (1 lb.)
Granulated Sugar
Vanilla
Baking Powder
Baking Soda
Yeast
Pectin

Frozen Pies of any kind (list)

Frozen Dinners (list kind & qty.)

Frozen Chicken

Frozen Hamburger or Beef

Frozen Lamb or Pork

Frozen Fish (list kind)

Ice Cream -
Sherbet -

Processed American Cheese
Other Cheeses & Cheese Food

Tea - Coffee - Cocoa

EXTRA BOOSTERS:
  Vitamins/Minerals

Items to Pre-Prepare or Purchase Ready-made:
Ice Cream Cakes (4)
Cranberry Muffins
Banana Bread
Date Nut Bread
Blueberry Muffins
Brownies
Cakes
Coffee Cake or Cozonac
  (optional; can buy at day-old)
Jelly and Jam (make great gifts ,too!)
Lasagne
Salad Dressings (can buy in bulk and
  share or use recipe for big savings)
Cookies (Chocolate Chip, Oatmeal,
  Bar Cookies, etc.)
Meatloaf (freeze in serving portions)
Hamburgers (freeze in portions)
Chicken (frozen, boneless breasts)
Cod; trout; frozen fish for chowder
Chili con carne (made in bulk)
Pies - Pumpkin (pre-prepared)
  Apple, Peach, Cherry, Boysenberry:
  (possibly buy frozen wholesale)
Your Personal Favorites:

List of Items to Buy Periodically:	Shopping Notes:
Milk Oranges Apples Bananas Oleo or Butter Mozarella Cheese Cottage Cheese Chipped Beef Cream Cheese Frankfurters Other Items You May Wish to Add	

Chapter 11. Sample Recipes—or Use Your Own
(Multiply by the Number of Families Networking Together)

WAFFLES MADE FROM SCRATCH
(or you may buy frozen or use a mix)
This is so easy that it didn't make any sense *not* to include this recipe: Sift together 2 cups, 3 tsp. baking powder, 1/2 tsp. salt, Separate 3 eggs and beat the whites until they're frothy but not dry. Gradually add 2-3 tablespoons sugar, and beat until egg whites peak softly. Beat yokes, add 1-3/4 cups milk and 1/4 cup melted margarine; combine quickly and lightly with flour mixture, then fold in egg whites. Bake in a hot waffle iron. Serve with syrup, butter, ice cream or fruit topping. Also delicious with mashed bananas or applesauce added to batter, but add a bit more flour.

TURKEY LEFTOVERS ON TOAST
Lightly saute diced onions, celery, parsley, sage, favorite seasonings with 2 cups of cubed cooked Turkey. Add separately cooked mixed vegetables (frozen variety) and a can of mushroom soup (undiluted) and, if you wish, pimentos (optional). Serve hot on toast points.

ICE CREAM CAKE
Bake a cake mix (your choice)—or use pound cake. When it's cool, slice through the middle lengthwise, and layer cake and ice cream. Frost generously with your favorite flavor icing. (Already prepared icings on the supermarket shelf will probably cover 1-1/2 to 2 ice cream cakes.) Box and seal, quick-freezing in the freezer.

CRANBERRY MUFFINS
Chop 1 c. cranberries, fresh or frozen. Mix with 1/3 c. sugar and 1/4 c. orange juice. Set aside. Beat 1 egg and 1 c. milk with mixer, add 1/4 c. vegetable oil or melted margarine. Sift 2 c. flour, 3 tsp. double-acting baking powder, and a pinch of salt; add to the liquids and mix just enough to moisten. Stir in cranberries lightly

(not too much mixing), and drop into muffin tins lined with paper muffin cups. Bake at 400° for 20-25 minutes. Makes 12-16 muffins. Cool; store in freezer ziplocks until you need them.

MACARONI, BEEF & TOMATO CASSEROLE
This is a cinch: Boil macaroni approx. 8-10 minutes till it's tender. Drain. Meanwhile saute a pound of hamburger meat and drain off the excess fat. Add your favorite seasonings, onion (unless the kids don't like it) and a can of tomato soup (undiluted). Combine with macaroni and serve. 4-6 generous servings.

STRAWBERRY SHORTCAKE
Follow the directions on the biscuit recipe box, split the fluffy biscuits and load on the strawberries! Whipped topping's nice, too.

DICED HAM & ESCALLOPED POTATOES
Prepare this for a crowd. Using your vegetable slicer, slice up a bunch of potatoes. (Peel if you want to, or keep all the vitamins next to the skins intact. Just make sure they're washed thoroughly with a vegetable brush.) Dice or cube a generous amount of ham, keeping the ratio about 1 to 2 (ham to potatoes). Partially cook the potatoes in water, drain, and reserve extra water to use in making white sauce (retains vitamins, too). Cook up a white sauce (it's nothing but a smidge of flour and margarine thickened together and blended to the right consistency using water and milk). When you're cooking for large numbers, make sure you make plenty of sauce! Season with parsley, paprika, pepper, melt some grated cheese into it, whatever you normally season your food with, and mix ham, potatoes and sauce together. Make up a bunch of well greased, oven-safe casserole dishes, cool, cover and seal. To serve, all you have to do is thaw, heat for 20 minutes and bring it to the table.

BREADS, ROLLS, COFFEE CAKE
For a pittance you can purchase all your monthly bread at a day-old bakery outlet. Freeze it and use as needed. (Face it: Most of

the bread at your grocery store is more than a day old. "Day-old" is just bread left over after deliveries that day at the store that charges you a fortune.)

HAM SLICES
By buying a 5# or 10# canned ham, a group can get enough ham slices and diced ham for casseroles for the entire month. Freeze in portions and quantities needed for different meals; thaw when needed.

BRAN MUFFINS
Ever buy bran cereal and wish you hadn't? Now you can get rid of it and still benefit your body! Stir approx. 1 c. whole bran (cereal or unprocessed bran flakes) into 1 c. milk and set aside for 15 minutes. Meanwhile sift 1-1/4 c. flour, 2 tsp. baking powder, and 1/2 tsp. salt. Unless you're using presifted flour, sift 2-3 times. Cream 1/2 stick of margarine with 1/4 c. sugar, then add 1 egg and beat thoroughly. Next add the bran-milk. Last add the flour mixture and mix just until it's lightly moistened. Line muffin tins with paper liners, fill 1/2 to 2/3 full and bake at 400° for 20-25 minutes. 12-16 muffins. Cool, freeze in ziplock bags.

DATE NUT BREAD
Chop up 12-16 oz. pitted dates and combine with 1-1/4 c. brown sugar, a stick of margarine and 1-1/2 c. boiling water. Set aside and let cool. Combine and sift together: 1-5/8 c. flour, 1 tsp. salt, and 2 tsp. baking soda. When the date mixture is cool, stir in 2 well beaten eggs. Then add flour mixture, 3-4 tsp. rum flavoring (optional) and 1 c. chopped pecans or walnuts. Makes two loaves in well greased loaf pans. Bake at 350° F. until done (50-60 minutes average baking time.) Test and if toothpick comes out clean, it's done. Cool on oven rack, then wrap in cellophane, place in large ziplock freezer bag.

STIR-FRY CHICKEN OVER RICE PILAF

Bring water to a boil, using twice as much water as rice. Throw in a bouillon cube, parsley, seasonings. When the water begins to simmer, add the rice, cover, lower the temperature under the pot and let simmer for 20 minutes until all the water is absorbed. At the same time, cook about a cup of frozen mixed vegetables. Then microwave-thaw 1 or 2 deboned chicken breasts and cut into bite size pieces. Saute chopped onion and green pepper, water chestnuts (canned is okay), fresh bean sprouts and miniature baby corn in a hot skillet with the chicken and soy sauce (optional—I don't care if you use catsup, just season to your family's personal taste). Add a tablespoon or two of water as needed. Cook just until the chicken is cooked through, but not tough, combining with other ingredients, including drained mixed vegetables. Add seasonings and serve over rice. Except for the rice, nothing takes more than 6-8 minutes to prepare.

INSTANT LEMON OR CHOCOLATE PUDDING

Followed the packaged directions. Pour into pretty serving dishes and refrigerate. It's ready in 5 minutes. (Handy dessert to prepare while you're waiting for water to boil, etc., for the rest of the meal.)

FRENCH TOAST

I know you can buy frozen French Toast, but my recipe is so cheap and fast, you've just got to try it: It's not fancy, just beaten eggs (add a tablespoon of milk, if you insist, but it's not necessary) and bread. Saturate the bread with the egg batter and drop on a hot greased skillet. Turn with spatula. Serve with syrup or powdered sugar and—Voila! Your family will think you're a genius. (Grab all the hugs you can get. You're worth it.)

MICROWAVED "BAKED" POTATOES

Wash potatoes. Jab a fork tine into each potato several times on each side (top and bottom). Cook in microwave for 3-4 minutes;

turn over and cook other side. Should "give" slightly when compressed. Serve with butter or margarine, salt, pepper, sour cream and chives (your choice).

BROILED COD (OR YOUR CHOICE OF FISH)
Thaw in refrigerator, so it's ready to place on broiler when you get home. Sprinkle with salt; brush with melted butter. Broil on one side, turn, brush with more butter, and broil other side, keeping a close eye on it. Takes very little time. Test degree of "doneness" with a fork. Serve right away with lemon, tartar sauce.

CHIPPED BEEF ON TOAST
Make white sauce, adding soft processed American cheese for additional nutrition and flavor, if you wish, shred two, three or four 2.5 oz. packages of chipped beef, depending on size of your family, and stir into the white sauce. Season to taste and serve on toast points. An inexpensive but delicious change of pace for either breakfast or a casual supper.

BAKED LASAGNA
This is another basic recipe you can prepare in advance and freeze. Cook as much lasagna pasta as you will need to create a three or four layer dish. While the pasta is cooking, grate 1 lb. mozzarella cheese, and combine with 1 lb. cottage cheese; set aside. Saute 1 lb. hamburger meat with chopped onions, celery, garlic, parsley, 3/4 tsp. oregano, and other Italian seasonings. Drain off excess fat. Combine meat with a large glass container of spaghetti sauce. (You decide whether to buy it with mushrooms and peppers, or not).

When the pasta is cooked but not mushy, drain and then fill the cook pot with cold water, so the pasta won't stick together, while you assemble the various ingredients. Grease your pan (two 8 X 8" squares or 9X13" pan for larger family). Ladle some meat sauce into the bottom, then a layer of pasta strips, then sprinkle the cheese mix, then another layer of pasta, then more meat sauce, then pasta,

and top with a generous amount of the cheese mix. Bake in a 350°
oven for approx. 30-40 minutes (till cheese melts). When ready,
serve with garlic bread and green tossed salad.

BAKED CHICKEN WITH STUFFING

Remove the giblets and neck from the body cavity. Rinse bird
thoroughly, salt the cavity and stuff bird just before putting it in the
oven. MOM'S SPECIAL STUFFING: This is the recipe my
children like so much, especially when I serve it with Turkey. It's
extremely simple, yet generations have used it since it was brought
over to this country years ago. from England. You'll never buy
expensive packaged stuffing again! Cut day-old bread in strips and
cube, then slow-dry for a few minutes in the oven (300°). (This is
an easy way to make croutons, by the way; just shake on a bit of
seasoning and melted butter before putting it in the oven.)

Meanwhile saute chopped onions, celery in butter or margarine.
Toss with toasted bread, sage, parsley, pepper, paprika, oregano or
rosemary, add 1-3/4 c. broth made with 1 or 2 bouillon cubes; stir
in one slightly beaten egg and a cup of raisins. Stuff the bird
lightly. Don't cram!

If you're stuffing a turkey: Stuff the neck with sage-flavored
pork sausage, just as it comes out of the wrapper. (It keeps the bird
moist throughout the baking time, and it's a delicious treat for the
children.) Also stuff any leftover bread stuffing under the skin on
either side of the breast, just above the legs; close the opening. Pour
a smidge of water in the bottom of the pan to create steam and to
mingle with the natural juices of the bird. Cover the breast bone
with stale bread. Cover the roasting pan and bake at 350° until it's
tender enough to fall apart. (Usually 20 min. per lb.) Occasionally
baste the bird to delay the skin crisping.

QUICK GRAVY TRICK: Drippings from the bird make
wonderful gravy, but sometimes you may want to extend its
marvelous flavor. Open a couple of cans of Cream of Chicken Soup
into a large skillet. Add the hot drippings, stir until it's the right
consistency. Serve with fowl, potatoes, rice or noodles.

MEAT, CHICKEN OR VEGETABLE POT PIES

Small pot pies are available in the frozen food section of your store, but most are big on gravy and skimpy on meat and vegetables. You will find pot pies handy and more satisfying if you use a good pie crust recipe, fill it with cooked vegetables, cubed meat and vegetables in a small amount of gravy, and top it with more crust. Here's a good pie pastry:
Crumble 5 c. sifted flour, 1 tablespoon brown sugar, 1 tsp. baking powder, 1 tsp. salt, and 1 lb. good quality lard i a large mixing bowl. Put 2 tablespoons vinegar in a measuring cup and fill to 2/3 c. with cold water. Add 1 egg and beat, then add to dry mixture. Divide into fist-sized balls and chill in refrigerator in plastic bags. Roll out and use as needed. Using this or another recipe of your choosing, you can improvise, pre-prepare and freeze delicious pot pies!

BANANA BREAD

Blend together 2/3 c. sugar and 1/3 c. margarine, add 2 eggs, then 3 tablespoons milk. Sift together 2 cups flour, 2 tsp. baking powder, 1/2 tsp. soda, and add to creamed batter. Then add 1 cup mashed bananas, 1/2 c. nuts, 1 tsp. vanilla. Fold in walnut bits, if you like. Bake at 350° in a greased loaf pan for approx. 50 minutes. Remove from oven when done, let stand 15 minutes, then remove from pan and cool on rack. When cool, wrap in cellophane and freeze in large ziplock bag. Double, triple for extra treats and nibbling during the holidays

CHOCOLATE FUDGE BROWNIES

Melt two sticks of margarine with 4 squares unsweetened bakers chocolate in the top of a double boiler (hot not boiling water in bottom pan). Sift 1-1/2 cups flour with 1 tsp. baking powder, 1/2 tsp. salt. Beat 4 eggs until they're fluffy yellow. Add 2 cups of sugar gradually to the eggs, stir in melted chocolate and 2 tsp. vanilla. Beat until blended thoroughly, then stir in flour mixture and 1 c. walnuts (optional). Spread in a greased 9X15 pan or two 8" square pans. Bake at 350° for 20-25 minutes. Remove from oven and score the surface lightly into squares with sharp knife. When they're cool, cut the brownies and wrap individually in cellophane, then bag and freeze in freezer bags.

MEATLOAF

Like most recipes, making meatloaf only requires good sense as to what belongs in it and what doesn't. You can add grated cheese or a small can of thoroughly drained spinach, for instance. What follows is a pretty basic recipe: Combine 1 to 1-1/2 lbs. meatloaf (depends on how many you're cooking for) with 3/4 c. oatmeal, an egg, a can of tomato soup (undiluted), and 1-2 tsp. bottled mustard, plus a little pepper, paprika, and season to suit your family's tastebuds. **To cut baking time in half,** form the meatloaf into portions the size of a child's fist and bake in a muffin tin for 20-25 minutes in a 350° F. oven . Naturally adults and teens will eat more than one, but for smaller children, it's just the right sized portion.

BISCUITS WITH TURKEY AND GRAVY

Biscuit mix takes 13-15 minutes to bake, while you dice up the last of the Thanksgiving turkey—which you froze right after deboning it, remember? Blend the turkey scraps into white sauce (1 tablespoons each of flour and margarine, add milk and (optional) a bit of grated or soft processed American cheese for a more robust flavor. Season and serve over open biscuits. A hearty way to start your family's engines some cold morning!

NO SUGAR BAKED APPLES

Core as many apples as needed, then stuff as many raisins as you can into the center. Place on plastic-wrap in the microwave and "bake" for 3-5 minutes until the apple skin is soft. A real treat for diabetics and others who want to avoid processed sugar, but have a sweet tooth.

HEARTY CLAM CHOWDER
You deserve a break today. Open two big soup cans of hearty clam chowder. Or get out the old cookbook. By the way, you can combine fish *and* clams for your own original secret recipe! A bit of crumbled crisp bacon adds flavor, too.

OMELETTE
With six eggs you can serve four people. You can either whip the whole egg, or separate and whip the whites till they're stiff, then fold gently into the beaten yokes. Careful handling and cooking slowly over a lower heat without much manipulation, is all that differentiates an omelette from scrambled eggs. Fold in chopped ham, cheese, vegetables.

IRISH STEW
(Adapt to Whatever Nationality You Wish)
Trim the fat off approx. 1-1/2 lbs. lamb or beef, dredge in a small amount of flour, sat and pepper, then saute in a skillet until lightly browned (to seal in the juices and flavor). Chop onions, celery, parsley, thyme, whatever herbs you wish; toss in with the meat. Split, then cut carrots into thin strips about 1-1/2" long. Add quartered potatoes and any root vegetables your family likes. For a Mediterranean touch, chopped tomatoes and peppers add flavor, vitamins and zest. Put all the meat, seasonings and vegetables into a crockpot, add enough water to barely cover everything, set the crockpot on the low setting, plug it in and go off to work. When you get back, all you do is *maybe* add more seasoning. Serve with bread or rolls, a tossed salad, and you've got a great meal.

COZONAC (Coffee Cake)
Melt three sticks of butter or margarine and set aside. Combine 2 cups milk and 1 cup sweet cream, then crush 2 cakes of yeast and add it to the milk mixture and let it dissolve. Blend in 1 c. sugar, a tsp. salt, and several cups of flour (keep adding flour gradually until the whole batter is moist and pliable). Add 8 egg

yolks. If the dough is too thin to handle, add more flour. Add cooled melted butter a little at a time and blend.

Keep adding flour until dough becomes springy and dry. Cover and set aside to rise in a warm spot. Cut into four equal parts and roll out each section on a floured board. Using a filling made up of 2 cups ground walnuts and 1 cup. ground-up raisins, sprinkle on dough rolled approx. 1/2" thick, then roll up and fold the ends together. Do this with each of the four portions of dough and place in well greased loaf pans. Let rise again approx. 20 minutes. Spread the top of each loaf with lightly beaten egg and bake at 325° F. for 45 minutes. Remove from the oven when it tests ready and is golden brown. [One year at Christmas I made the mistake of going to bed, trusting my husband to do the honors. Dutifully he turned off the oven, but left the beautifully baked loaves in the oven. The next morning they were hard as bricks!] Done right, these make terrific gifts and make for delicious snacking. Cool on a rack, then freeze until needed.

Before serving, you can add a simple icing (optional) made by creaming 2 tablespoons margarine with 1/2 tsp. vanilla, 1-1/2 tablespoons milk, and 1 c. sifted powdered sugar. Serve with your favorite beverages and enjoy all that lovely Christmas cheer!

CREPES A` LA RUMANIA

This isn't on the 30-Day Menu Plan, but you may want to try it for a special Christmas Eve treat. My Rumanian in-laws gave me this recipe, and it's infallibly delicious. Your only problem will be keeping up with the demand for more! Combine 1 c. sifted flour, a pinch of salt, and a tablespoon of sugar in a deep mixing bowl. Add 4 eggs one at a time and continue to mix until all the eggs have been blended with the flour mixture. Then pour in 1 c. milk gradually, mixing all the while, until it's thoroughly mixed and the batter is thin and smooth. Add a tsp. water and beat until it is thin enough to spread like a tissue when you pour it into the skillet. Follow the order I've given you, and you will get a perfect batter every time with no lumps. Add a tsp. of vanilla. This takes only minutes to mix, and you can store it in the refrigerator for a few hours before using, if you wish.

When you pour the batter slowly into a hot buttered skillet, tip and swirl the pan. Your wrist action will spread the tissue-thin pancake batter more quickly. As soon as it spreads out the size of a small dinner plate, flip it over and quickly fry the other side. Remove from the frying pan and continue to fry as many as your family can consume

Suggestion: Have someone else spread each crepe as it comes from the skillet, using grape jelly or shredded cheese (depending on whether you want sweet or cheesy crepes). Just a little jelly or cheese is needed; then roll each crepe so that it can be picked up and eaten with the fingers, kid-style, or with a fork. A dollop of sour cream makes these even more delicious. When you're cooking for a crowd, you will want to use two or three frying pans, and be prepared to work fast, since it only takes a few seconds for each side to cook. The compliments you will receive will reward you for your time and effort.

CHICKEN AND HAM STRIPS EN CASSEROLE

Improvise. Cut a chicken breast and a small ham steak (or a couple of sandwich ham slices) in strips, saute with chopped green peppers, onions, and grated carrots. Serve over noodles, rice, or combine with a cream sauce (mushroom soup is a quick method) and sliced potatoes for a nice variation on escalloped potatoes. The protein and great taste make this dish disappear fast!

POTATO PANCAKES

This recipe calls for a small amount of freshly extracted onion juice. For a minimum of tears, use a blender to extract a small amount of juice from approx. half a slice of onion. Easy does it! Subtlety in cooking always is appreciated. Once you have a measurable 1/4 tsp. of juice (discard any pulp), combine with 4 beaten eggs and 2 c. milk. Next add to this mixture 1/2 c. pre-sifted flour, 4 tsp. double-acting baking powder, and 1-1/2 tsp. salt. Beat this batter until smooth; then gently add 6 cups grated uncooked potatoes (7-8 potatoes). Ladle onto a hot greased griddle and fry until crisp and golden, then turn and cook the other side. Serve with applesauce or sour cream.

CREAMED SHRIMP
Combine approx. 2 lbs. fresh frozen shrimp (bought in bulk, of course) with 2-1/2 cups of white sauce, mushrooms, and sliced olives (I prefer black, but green ones also work well). Serve over rice.

CARROT-PINEAPPLE SALAD
Combine grated carrots and crushed pineapple. Simple and fast.

MUD PIE
There are more complicated recipes. Here's one I like for its simplicity: Crush half a package of Nabisco chocolate wafers and blend with 1/2 stick of margarine, then press into the bottom of a 9" pie pan. Load on a quart of softened coffee ice cream. Put into freezer until ice cream is firm, then drizzle the top with cold fudge sauce and return to freezer until ready to serve. (Some people alternate layers of coffee and chocolate ice cream; depends on what you like!) Top with whipped cream and slivered almonds.

CHILI CON CARNE (An Ideal Co-op Recipe)
Wash and soak 1 lb. red chili beans overnight. Add 1-1/2 tsp. salt and enough water to cover the swollen beans. Cover and simmer until the beans are soft but not mushy. Remove from heat and let them cool; as they cool, more moisture will be absorbed. Save any excess liquid and boil separately so it will be concentrated. Meanwhile saute 2 lbs. lean hamburger meat a large chopped sweet onion and 3/4 c. celery. Drain off fat, add a sprinkling of 2-3 tablespoons flour, 3-1/2 cups tomato puree or freshly cooked, sieved tomatoes, 1 tablespoon chili powder, 1 tablespoon salt, a pinch of red cayenne pepper, 1 tsp. sugar, and 2 tsp. cider vinegar.

Heat and stir over a low fire until the mixture thickens, then add to the beans and 1 cup bean-liquid. Simmer for a few more minutes, and serve. (Divide up a "vat" of chili and freeze in meal size quantities for the families involved.)

ROAST DUCK WITH SAUERKRAUT DRESSING

Serve duck for a succulent change, if you like, from the traditional Christmas turkey. Remove giblets. Rub 1 tablespoon baking soda into the skin and thoroughly rinse the bird inside and out with warm water. Sprinkle inside and out with salt. Saute 3/4 c. onions and 1/2 c. celery in half a stick of butter or margarine. Drain a large can of sauerkraut and save the liquid. Add the sauerkraut, a tsp. caraway seed, and two pared, diced apples to the onions and butter, mixing well. Fill the cavity of the duck and sew shut. Place any leftover stuffing in the roasting pan around the duck and stick the giblets into the dressing, cover and bake at 350° F. about 3 hours in all. This will give you plenty of time to enjoy the Christmas service with your church family.

When you return home, uncover the duck to brown it during the last hour of cooking, while the table is set, and potatoes cooked and mashed. Or try wild rice—scrumptious! Gravy can be made with pan drippings and the sauerkraut juice you set aside; thicken with a little flour.

BEET BREAD

Even people who aren't crazy about beets will like this bread. (Remember, sugar comes from beets; the sweetness combined with herbs is fantastic!) Take a basic yeast recipe for bread, preferably a two loaf recipe. Use a cup of beef juice in lieu of some of the liquids. After the batter is well mixed, add your favorite herbs, such as dill, rosemary, thyme, and sage—sparingly, of course! As the dough rises (twice), the flavors will permeate the bread. This is fabulous with turkey breast sandwiches. The bread is a beautiful holiday pink. Nobody will ever guess what makes it look and taste so grand—unless you tell them.